|bulldog

understanding and
caring for your breed

Written by
Beverley Stephenson

bulldog

understanding and
caring for your breed

Written by
Beverley Stephenson

Pet Book Publishing Company

The Old Hen House, St Martin's Farm, Zeals, Warminster, Wiltshire, BA12 6NZ.

Printed and bound in South Korea.

ISBN: 978-1-910488-26-3

Acknowledgements

The publishers would like to thank the following for help with photography: Malcolm Presland and Melanie Vincent (Kofyn). Photo on page 27: Kofyn Kudja Wudja owned and bred by Malcolm Presland and Melanie Vincent, taken by Tracy Morgan Animal Photography (www. animalphotographer.co.uk)

Contents

Introducing the Bulldog

The Bulldog may be the ugly mug of the dog world, but there is scarcely any other breed that has such a devoted fan club. He has evolved from his days as a fearless bull baiter to become the most loyal and affectionate of companions.

Physical Characteristics

There is no mistaking the Bulldog for any other breed; he is truly unique and it is a case of once seen, never forgotten. Strong and muscular, the Bulldog is low in stature but his physique is broad, powerful and compact. His back is short, rising from the shoulders and then curving down towards a short tail which may be straight or screwed. The Bulldog moves with a characteristic, rolling gait – another breed speciality.

His head is his outstanding feature, with his short muzzle, flattened nose, undershot jaw and heavy, overhanging flews (lips). His dark, round eyes have a stoical expression, but also one which says: "don't mess with me".

He has a smooth, short coat which comes in a variety of colours – reds, fawns, brindles, white and pied colours (white with patches of colour) – and these should be pure and brilliant.

What is a brachycephalic breed?

This is the name given to breeds that have a foreshortened muzzle and a flattened nose. As well as the Bulldog, other brachycephalic breeds include the Pug, the Boxer, the French Bulldog and the Pekingese.

This type of head construction looks highly distinctive but it should never be exaggerated as it can have an adverse effect on health and wellbeing. The short muzzle and pushed back nose can lead to difficulties with breathing. The superficial sign of this are the snores that will, undoubtedly, emanate from your Bulldog, but on a more serious note, he may suffer from laboured breathing, particularly in hot weather.

Temperament

The Bulldog has its origins as a fighting dog (see Tracing Back, page14) but he has left this legacy far behind and is now regarded as one of the most outstanding of companion dogs. He is often referred to as the British Bulldog, not just because he is a British breed, but because he embodies the British character: tough, gritty, determined and loyal. He also has a wicked sense of humour, and seems to delight in playing the clown. He is quite a complex character and the Breed Standard, which is a written blueprint for the breed, gives a detailed breakdown of the ideal temperament.

According to the Standard, the Bulldog should be:

- Alert: The Bulldog takes a lively interest in everything that is going on, but there are times when he is sleeping (and snoring...) when he is clearly saying: "do not disturb!"

- Bold: This dates back to the Bulldog's history as a bull baiter and, to this day he shows great confidence and self-assurance.

Below: A short muzzle and and a flat nose are typical features of the Bracycephalic breeds.

- Loyal: This is an integral part of the Bulldog's character and is the prime reason why he is so highly valued as a companion dog.

- Dependable: A reliable dog with a sound temperament that can be trusted in all situations is worth his weight in gold.

- Courageous: Again, a throwback to his days as a bullfighter. This quality is rarely tested, but most Bulldogs have a quiet confidence and will give a good account of themselves if challenged.

Fierce in appearance but possessed of an affectionate nature: What a delightful combination! The Bulldog looks like a mini tank, but inside that tough exterior is a sweet-natured dog that is lavish with his gifts of love and affection.

Living with a Bulldog

The Bulldog is an adaptable dog and will fit in with most family situations. He adores children and will bring a huge amount of pleasure to the family circle, but he will also be an entertaining companion for older people.

He is equally happy in the town or in the country, and will scarcely notice whether you have a mansion or a small apartment – with the proviso that he doesn't have to climb many stairs....

The Bulldog is not the most energetic of breeds. Adolescents may go through a more turbulent time, but most adults will be content with moderate exercise, which means they can fit in with many different lifestyles. One word of warning: the male is bigger and stronger than the female, and he can be a bit of a handful while he is growing up. This means that the Bulldog – particularly a male Bulldog – may not be the best choice for anyone who is frail or infirm.

That said, the Bulldog has so few drawbacks as a breed, it is little wonder that he is growing in popularity. After all, who can resist the unique charm of a dog that looks like a battleaxe on the outside, but on the inside is kind and gentle!

Below: Rest and relaxation come high on the Bulldog's list of priorities.

Tracing back in time

The Bulldog, the most amiable of animals, has come a long way from his days as a fierce guard and courageous bull-baiter. But throughout his long history there is a common thread - the Bulldog has always been highly valued by his human owners for his steadfast loyalty.

The ancestors of Bulldogs are thought to trace back to the days of ancient Greece when fierce Molossian hounds were prized for their hunting skills.

These dogs had strong, compact bodies and short faces – features which are recognisable in today's Bulldog.

All things of value were traded in the Mediterranean region, and it is thought that Phoenician traders introduced Molossian hounds to Britain around 600 BC.

They were used for their hunting skills, but also found a role as war dogs and guard dogs. Strabo, a contemporary of Julius Caesar, in his description of Britain in 63-64 BC, wrote:

"It produces corn, cattle, gold, silver and iron, which also forms its exports together with skins slaves and dogs of a superior breed for the chase. The Gauls use these dogs in war, as well as others of their own breed."

Bull Baiting

Originally the name 'Mastiff' did not apply to a specific breed as it does today. It was the name given to a group of large, general-purpose dogs, distinct from spaniels, hounds and toy dogs.

There are reports of dogs of this type being used for bear baiting, as well as a breed, now extinct, known as the Alaunt, which was famed for his speed, strength and ferocity.

When the sport of bull baiting became popular in the 13th century, it was a combination of these breed types that proved most successful.

But soon fanciers realised that a smaller dog who could fly at the bull's head and grab his nose, or any part of his face, in his powerful jaws could bring a bull down and pin it.

In the 17th century dogs were bred specifically for the sport of bull baiting.

Selective breeding produced the Bulldog, the perfect dog for the job. He is described as:

"...low in stature, but strong and muscular and probably the most courageous creature in the world"

Soon there were bullrings in all the major market towns in Britain; big crowds came to view the spectacle and gambling was fierce. The Bulldog's courage was legendary.

In his book The Dog, written in 1872, Idstone observed that although the dogs were small and low when once they seized the bull's throat "you might sooner cut them in pieces than make them let go their hold". However, the sport of bull bating came at a price. Many dogs were killed ... "the bull tossing them up in the air like footballs."

End of an Era

In 1835, the Humane Act Of Parliament abolished the baiting of bulls and bears and dog fighting in public. This signalled the end of the bullring as a place of entertainment, replaced by the undercover world of dog fighting. The dog pit required a smaller, faster, more agile dog, and so Bulldogs were interbred with terriers to produce the Bull Terrier and the Staffordshire Bull Terrier. So what was to become of the loyal Bulldog, once Britain's greatest crowd-pleaser and now redundant?

Thankfully, the days of the Bulldog as a fighting breed are buried in the past.

Developing the breed

The Bulldog was no longer needed to bait bulls, but enthusiasts were determined that this loyal, affectionate and distinctly British dog should not be lost.

A new sport – dog showing – was emerging, with the first official show staged in 1859. The following year, the Birmingham show offered classes for Bulldogs, and so there was a new incentive to keep the breed alive. In 1864 the first Bulldog Club was formed, but this proved to be short-lived.

There was a temporary replacement in 1874 but it was the next year, 1875, that the Bulldog Club was born. Breeders met together and decided on rules and regulations but, most importantly, they worked on a Breed Standard, a written description of what the ideal Bulldog should look like. The Bulldog Club is still in existence today and it has the distinction of being the oldest breed club in the world.

The First Champion

The breed's first Champion was Ch. Old King Dick, owned by Jacob Lamphier of Sheffield. He was a red smut dog, weighing 22kg (48lb). He won his title at the Birmingham show in 1865 and was a universal favourite with judges throughout his illustrious career.

Sadly this was cut short in heartbreaking circumstances, which sum up the Bulldog character. Old Dick's owner, Jacob Lamphier fell ill with tuberculosis and for the last 12 months of his life he was confined to his room with Old King Dick as his constant companion.

When Jacob died, Old King Dick was distraught, searching for him from room to room, and eventually lying down on a rug in front of the fire in sad resignation. From that moment he never lifted his head again; he refused all food and died four days after the death of his beloved master.

The Legacy

Ch. Old King Dick's memory lived on in his progeny, many of whom proved to be top-quality show dogs. His most influential descendent was a dog called Ch. Crib, also known as Sheffield Crib, who was bred by Jacob Lamphier's son.

Facing page: Ch.Old King Dick: A great show dog and an outstanding companion.

Crib was a brindle and white dog, weighing a hefty 29kg (64lb). He was born in 1871 and was never beaten in the show ring. At the Bulldog Club shows in 1892 and 1893, he figured in the pedigree of every Bulldog entered and was ultimately responsible for establishing the four main strains of the breed.

Bulldogs in the USA

British settlers to the New World took their dogs with them, and this included the Bulldog. The first record is of a dog called Donald sent over by Irish exhibitor, Sir William Verner, to take part in the 1880 New York show. Other early show dogs included Noble and Bonnie Boy, but more quality was needed. Col. John E. Thayer, the first president of the Bulldog Club of America, was passionate about the breed and he made significant imports from England, which included Blister and Robinson Crusoe from George Raper and Britomartis from Ron S. Barlow. With enhanced bloodlines, the breed went from strength to strength and by 1893, three years after the formation of the Bulldog Club of America, entries were up 50 per cent on the previous year. The breed was here to stay.

The current scene

The British Bulldog has universal appeal and is well established in many countries throughout the world. In the UK the number of registrations is increasing, and there are significant Bulldog populations in Europe, Japan, South America and the USA. Now that the priority is to produce healthy Bulldogs without exaggeration, the breed's future looks bright.

What should a Bulldog look like?

The Bulldog, with his thick set, low slung body, and his massive short-faced head has attracted a worldwide fan club. So what makes a Bulldog so special?

Every pedigree breed has a Breed Standard, which is a written blueprint describing how a dog should look, how he should move, and what his temperament should be like. If adhered to by breeders, dogs of recognisable breed type will be produced, with the correct characteristics and temperament.

The Breed Standard has significance beyond the sport of showing for it is the dogs that win in the ring that will be used for breeding. The winners of today are therefore responsible for passing on their genes to future generations and preserving the breed in its best form. This has major significance at the present

time when governing bodies are encouraging breeders to produce Bulldogs without exaggeration, putting health and the ability to function above the dictates of fashion. The aim is to produce a typical Bulldog, with all the charm that is so strongly associated with the breed, but avoiding the pitfalls of breeding dogs that are adversely affected by their conformation.

General appearance

The Bulldog is a powerfully built, compact dog that is somewhat low in stature. His head is large in proportion to his body, but not so much as to destroy the general symmetry. He should convey an impression of determination, strength and activity. He has a broad, short muzzle, but this should not interfere with his breathing – a stipulation emphasised in the British Standard. Females are not so grand or well developed as males.

Temperament

The Bulldog temperament is multi-faceted, giving him unique appeal. Dating back to his bull-fighting ancestry, he is courageous, bold and alert. But coupled with this is his intense loyalty. He is loving and affectionate and goes through life with a calm, self-assured sense of his own dignity.

Points of anatomy

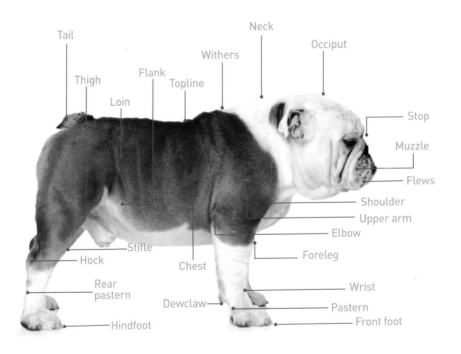

Tail

Thigh

Loin

Flank

Topline

Withers

Neck

Occiput

Stop

Muzzle

Flews

Shoulder

Upper arm

Elbow

Foreleg

Stifle

Hock

Chest

Rear pastern

Dewclaw

Wrist

Pastern

Hindfoot

Front foot

Head and skull

The Bulldog head is the outstanding characteristic of the breed, and both the British and the American Standards give detailed descriptions as to what the perfect Bulldog head should look like.

The skull is relatively large in circumference and measures at least the same as the height of the dog at the shoulders. The forehead is flat, with finely wrinkled skin; the cheeks are well developed, extending sideways beyond the eyes.

The stop, the step-up between the muzzle and the forehead, is defined; the face from the front of the cheekbone to the nose is relatively short and may be slightly wrinkled. The muzzle is short and broad, turning upwards. The nose and the nostrils are large, broad and black in colour. A dog with a brown or liver-coloured nose would be disqualified in the American show ring.

The Bulldog may have a nose-roll, a fold of skin above the nose, and this may be full or split. In the interests of the dog's health and his ability to breath, an exaggerated nose roll is considered highly undesirable.

The flews (chops) are thick, broad and deep, covering the lower jaw at both sides. Teeth should not be visible.

Eyes

When looking at a Bulldog front-on, the eyes are situated low down the skull, well away from the ears. They are positioned wide apart and should be in a straight line with the stop. They are round in shape, and should be neither prominent nor sunken. When looking forward, no white of the eye should be visible. The colour is very dark – almost black.

Ears

The ears are set high almost as if they were on the top corners of the skull. They are placed wide apart and as far from the eyes as possible. Small and thin, the 'rose-shaped' ears fold backwards to display part of the inside ear.

Mouth

The jaws are broad and square, and the bite is undershot, with the lower jaw projecting in front of the upper jaw. The teeth are large and strong, with the canine teeth (tusks) set well apart and the six, small teeth between the canines set in an even, level row.

Neck

The neck is moderate in length, thick, deep and strong. It should be well-arched at the back with some loose skin about the throat, forming a dewlap (a loose, fold of skin) on either side.

Forequarters

The shoulders are broad, sloping and deep. They are very muscular and powerful and give the impression of being tacked on to the body. The elbows are low and stand well out from the body. The chest is wide, prominent and deep.

Body

The back is short and strong, broad at the shoulders and comparatively narrow at the loins.

A breed characteristic is a roach back; this is seen as a fall in the topline behind the shoulders, rising to the loins (which are higher than the shoulders) and curving more suddenly to the tail, forming a slight arch.

The ribcage is well-rounded and deep, giving the dog a broad, short-legged appearance.

Hindquarters

The back legs are large and muscular and are slightly longer than the front legs. The stifles ('knees') turn very slightly away from the body, the hocks ('ankles') are slightly bent.

Movement

The Bulldog has a unique way of moving with short, quick steps on the tips of his toes. The

Facing page: The expression which comes from the Bulldog's eyes is one of calm assurance.

hind feet appear to skim the ground. It is the peculiar conformation of the Bulldog – his wide-set front legs, narrow loin and longer rear legs – which produce the characteristic 'rolling' gait. Good conformation results in sound movement; poor conformation will, inevitably, produce poor movement.

Feet

The feet are compact and moderate in size. The toes are well split up with high knuckles and short, stubby nails.

Tail

The British Standard calls for a straight tail, whereas the American Standard states that tails may be either straight or screwed. The screwed tail is considered undesirable on health grounds, particularly if it is tightly screwed. With selective breeding, screw tails may disappear but this will take some time.

The current requirement is for a straight tail that is set low. It should jut out a little and then turn downwards.

A high tail set is considered a fault as this would result in the tail being carried above the line of the back. It is moderate in length – more short than long – and in terms of shape, it is thick at the root tapering quickly to a fine point.

Coat

The Bulldog is smooth-coated with fine-textured, straight hair that lies close to the body. The coat should have a glossy appearance.

Colour

The pure, brilliant colour of the coat is a feature of the breed. The Bulldog may be solid-coloured or piebald – white with patches of colour, which should be symmetrically distributed.

All colours are equally acceptable in the UK, but the American Standard declares a preference for colours in the following order:

- Red brindle

- All other brindles

- Solid white

- Solid red, fawn or fallow

- Piebald

In the British show ring solid black is highly undesirable, but the American Standard states that this is not so objectionable if it occurs in brindle patches.

Size

The British Bulldog is a larger dog than his American counterpart. In the UK, the ideal weight for males is 25kg (55lb) and 23kg (50lb) for females. In the US, a mature male weighs around 23kg (50lb) and a female is 18kg (40lb). With increased awareness of health issues, heavyweight Bulldogs that exceed the size stipulations of the Breed Standard will not be favoured in the show ring.

Summing Up

Although the majority of Bulldogs are kept as pet dogs and will never be exhibited in the show ring, it is important that breeders strive for perfection and try to produce dogs that adhere as closely as possible to the Breed Standard.

This has become particularly important with the Bulldog, where exaggeration has led to very real health issues. Breeders need to retain all that is unique in this very special breed, but the top priority must be to produce typical examples of the breed that are sound in mind and body.

The Bulldog should not be too much of a heavyweight as this can be prejudicial to his health.

What do you want from your Bulldog?

There are over 200 dog breeds to choose from, so how can you be sure that the Bulldog is the right breed for you? Before you take the plunge into Bulldog ownership, you need to be 100 per cent confident that this is the breed that is best suited to your lifestyle.

Companion

The Bulldog's *raison d'être* in life is to be with people and so he is the perfect family companion. He is intensely loyal, and cares deeply about all members of his family circle. He may be more respectful of the grown ups, but children are of equal importance to him. He is loving and affectionate – and also very tolerant. This laid back canine takes life as it comes and, once mature, feels no real need to push his luck. These qualities are perfect for many different types of owner, but if you are highly energetic and want a long-distance walking companion, you will need to think again.

A fit Bulldog will enjoy taking exercise – but nothing overrides his love of creature comforts. Lazing around at home, surrounded by his loved ones, is his top priority – so make sure you share his outlook on life!

Sports dog

There are lots of canine sports to choose from, but if this is an area that interests you, the Bulldog may not be the breed for you.

His conformation does not lend itself to demanding speed sports. He is certainly clever, but he is not highly motivated to perform tasks without good reason.

However, with kindly, consistent training, you will make headway, and even though your Bulldog may not be a world-beater, you will be interacting with him and spending quality time with him, which will enhance your relationship.

For information on dog sports, see page 154.

Show dog

Do you have ambitions to exhibit your Bulldog in the show ring? This is a highly competitive sport, with sizeable entries at the big shows, so you do need the right dog to begin with.

If you plan to show your Bulldog you will have to track down a show quality puppy, and train him to perform in the show ring.

He has to learn how to show himself off to advantage and accept the detailed 'hands on' examination that he will be subjected to when being judged.

It is also important to bear in mind that not every puppy with show potential develops into a top-quality specimen. You must, therefore, be prepared to love your Bulldog and give him a home for life, even if he doesn't make the grade.

What does your Bulldog want from you?

A dog cannot speak for himself, so we need to view the world from a canine perspective and work out what a Bulldog needs in order to live a happy, contented and fulfilling life.

Time and commitment

First of all, a Bulldog needs a commitment that you will care for him for the duration of his life – guiding him through his puppyhood, enjoying his adulthood, and being there for him in his later years. If all potential owners were prepared to make this pledge, there would be scarcely any dogs in rescue.

The Bulldog's place is in the heart of the family and he will be thoroughly miserable if he is excluded

from family activities or has to spend long stretches of time on his own. A dog should not be left for longer than four hours at a stretch, and if you cannot fulfil this obligation, you would be wise to delay taking on a dog of any breed until your situation changes.

Practical matters

On the practical front, the Bulldog is a relatively easy breed to care for. He needs minimal grooming, and once you have found a diet that suits him, there should be no problems with feeding him. Exercise is often neglected as the laid back Bulldog will not demand to be taken out and some can be positively lazy. However, it is your responsibility to keep your Bulldog fit and healthy. A routine of varied exercise will be good for him physically and it will also provide mental stimulation as he investigates the world around him.

Leadership

The Bulldog is a loyal and affectionate dog and rarely feels the need to be pushy. However, he needs to understand his place in the family and respect all family members – big and small. This is all about building a relationship based on trust – and this starts from the moment your Bulldog arrives in your home. You are a benevolent leader, providing food and shelter. In addition, you set the boundaries and, as long as you are consistent so your Bulldog understands what is expected of him, he will be content to abide by the rules.

If you fail to do this, your Bulldog will have no option but to invent his own agenda and will be resentful if you try to impose your will. The secret is to start as you mean to go on: be a kind, caring and consistent leader and you will be rewarded with a companion that is second to none.

Your Bulldog needs to understand his place in the family circle.

Extra considerations

Now you have decided that a Bulldog is the dog of your dreams, you can narrow your choice so you know exactly what you are looking for.

Male or female?

Whether you choose a male or a female is a matter of personal preference. Bulldogs are very much individuals and so there are no hard and fast rules about temperamental differences between the genders. However, there are a few generalisations which are worth noting.

The male is physically bigger and stronger than the female and he has more presence. He can be headstrong, particularly when young and adolescent but, with guidance, he will mature into a loyal and loving companion.

A female Bulldog cares deeply about her home and family, and she can be protective. This is OK in moderation, but it is not behaviour that should be encouraged. Female Bulldogs do not always get on well together, and if there is a fall out – even between a mother and daughter – it can result in on-going problems. This is worth considering if you are adding to your Bulldog family.

If you opt for a female, you will need to cope with her seasons, which will start at around eight months of age and occur approximately every nine months thereafter. During the three-week period of a season, you will need to keep your bitch away from entire males (males that have not been neutered) to eliminate the risk of an unwanted pregnancy. Some owners also report that females may be a little moody and withdrawn during their seasonal cycle. Many pet owners opt for neutering, which puts an end to the seasons, and also has many attendant health benefits. The operation, known as spaying, is usually carried out at some point after the first season. The best plan is to seek advice from your vet.

An entire male may not cause many problems, although some do have a stronger tendency to mark, which could include the house.

However, training will usually put a stop to this. An entire male will also be on the lookout for bitches in season, and this may lead to difficulties, depending on your circumstances. Neutering (castrating) a male is a relatively simple operation, and there are associated health benefits. Again, you should seek advice from your vet.

Colour?

The Bulldog comes in a variety of colours ranging from white through a range of fawns to red. In terms of markings, Bulldogs may be brindled or pied – a white dog with coloured patches. If you are exhibiting your Bulldog in the show ring, you will be looking for more symmetrical markings and in the US some colours are considered more desirable than others (see page 34), but for the pet owner colour is purely a matter of personal preference.

More than one?

Bulldogs can be addictive, and you may decide that

two dogs would suit your lifestyle, and would be company for each other. As noted above, females do not always get on well together so bear this in mind if you are adding to your Bulldog population. Regardless of what sex you choose, do not fall into the trap of getting two puppies from the same litter, or even two of a similar age.

The two puppies will have no problem with the plan; they will always have someone to play with. But this could be at the cost of forming a proper bond with members of their human family.

You also need to consider the effect that rearing two puppies will have on your life. Looking after one puppy is hard work, but taking on two pups at the same time is more than double the workload.

House training is a nightmare as, often, you don't even know which puppy is making mistakes, and training is impossible unless you separate the two puppies and give them one-on-one attention.

 Be very wary of a breeder who encourages you to buy two puppies from the same litter, as it is unlikely that the welfare of the puppies is their top priority. Most responsible breeders have a waiting list of potential purchasers before a litter is even born and have no need to make this type of sale.

If you do decide to add to your Bulldog population, wait at least 18 months so your first dog is fully trained and settled before taking on a puppy.

An older dog

You may decide to miss out on the puppy phase and take on an older dog instead. Such a dog may be harder to track down, but sometimes a breeder will

rehome a female when her breeding career is at an end so she will enjoy the benefits of getting more individual attention. In some cases, the breeder may have run on a puppy as potential breeding stock and then found he/she is not suitable for this role, but will still make an excellent pet dog.

There are advantages to taking on an older dog, as you know exactly what you are getting. But the upheaval of changing homes can be quite upsetting, so you will need to have plenty of patience during the settling in period.

Rehoming a rescued dog

It is rare to find a Bulldog in an all breed rescue shelter. However, breed clubs run their own rescue schemes, and this is where you will find dogs that have failed to thrive in their first homes. Sometimes a dog needs to be rehomed through no fault of his own, mostly when a family's circumstances change.

The reasons are various, ranging from illness or death of the original owner to family breakdown, changing jobs, or even the arrival of a new baby. Occasionally, a Bulldog may not have received the all-important training, which every dog needs, and he may have become too much for his family to cope with.

This is unusual as the Bulldog is generally easy to

live with, but it could be that an individual, left to his own devices, has become too headstrong, or he may have developed anxieties if he has not been properly socialised.

If you decide you want to take on a rescued Bulldog, try to find out as much as you can about the dog's history so you know exactly what you are taking on. You need to be aware of his age and health status, his likes and dislikes, plus any behavioural issues that may be relevant.

You need to be realistic about what you are capable of achieving so you can be sure you can give the dog in question a permanent home.

Regardless of the dog's previous history, you will need to give him plenty of time and be patient with him as he settles into his new home. It may take weeks, or even months before he becomes fully integrated in the family, but if all goes well you will have the reward of knowing that you have given a Bulldog a second chance.

Sourcing a puppy

Your aim is to find a healthy puppy that is typical of the breed, and has been reared with the greatest possible care. Where to start?

A tried and trusted method of finding a puppy is to attend a dog show where your chosen breed is being exhibited. This will give you the opportunity to see a wide range of Bulldogs of different colours and different ages. If you look closely, you will also become aware of different 'types' on show. They are all purebred Bulldogs, but breeders produce dogs with a family likeness, so you can see which type you prefer.

When judging has been completed, talk to the exhibitors and find out more about their dogs. They may not have puppies available, but most will be planning a litter, and you may decide to put your name on a waiting list.

Bear in mind that breeding Bulldogs can be problematical, and there is a higher incidence of caesareans than in other breeds. For this reason, breeders limit the number of litters they produce, which often means lengthy waiting lists. This can be frustrating but if you have decided that a Bulldog is the breed for you, you must be prepared to be patient – it will be worth it in the end!

Internet research

The Internet is an excellent resource, but when it comes to finding a puppy, use it with care:

DO go to the website of your national Kennel Club.

Both the American Kennel Club (AKC) and the Kennel Club (KC) have excellent websites which will give you information about the Bulldog as a breed, and what to look for when choosing a puppy. You will also find contact details for specialist breed clubs (see below).

Both sites have lists of puppies available, and you can look out for breeders of merit (AKC) and assured breeders (KC) which indicates that a code of conduct has been adhered to.

DO find details of specialist breed clubs.

On breed club websites you will find lots of useful

information that will help you to care for your Bulldog. There may be contact details of breeders in your area, or you may need to go through the club secretary.

Some websites also have a list of breeders that have puppies available. The advantage of going through a breed club is that members will follow a code of ethics, and this will give you some guarantees regarding breeding stock and health checks.

If you are planning to show your Bulldog you will obviously want to go to a breeder that has had some success in the ring. You will need to do additional research to discover more about their breeding lines and the type of Bulldog they produce.

DO NOT look at puppies for sale.

There are legitimate Bulldog breeders with their own websites, and they may, occasionally, advertise a litter, although in most cases reputable breeders have waiting lists for their puppies.

The danger comes from unscrupulous breeders who produce puppies purely for profit, with no thought for the health of the dogs they breed from and no care given to rearing the litter.

Photos of puppies are hard to resist, but never make a decision based purely on an advertisement. You need to find out who the breeder is, and have the opportunity to visit their premises and inspect the litter before making a decision.

Questions, questions, questions

When you find a breeder with puppies available, you will have lots of questions to ask. These should include the following:

- Where have the puppies been reared? Hopefully, they will be in a home environment which gives them the best possible start in life.

- How many are in the litter?

- What is the split of males and females?

- What colours are available?

- How many have already been spoken for? The breeder will almost certainly be keeping a puppy to show or for breeding, and there may well be others on a waiting list.

- Can I see the mother with her puppies?

- What age are the puppies?

- When will they be ready to go to their new homes?

Bear in mind puppies need to be with their mother and siblings until they are eight weeks of age otherwise they miss out on vital learning and communication skills, which will have a detrimental effect on them for the rest of their lives.

You should also be prepared to answer a number of searching questions so the breeder can check if you are suitable as a potential owner of one of their precious puppies.

You will be asked some or all of the following questions:

- What is your home set up?

- Do you have children/grandchildren?

- What are their ages?

- Is there somebody at home the majority of the time?

- What is your previous experience with dogs?

- Do you have plans to show your Bulldog?

The breeder is not being intrusive; they need to understand the type of home you will be able to provide in order to make the right match. Do not be offended by this; the breeder is doing it for both the dog's benefit and also for yours.

Steer clear of a breeder who does not ask you questions. He or she may be more interested in making money out of the puppies rather than ensuring that they go to good homes. They may also have taken other short cuts which may prove disastrous, and very expensive, in terms of vet bills or plain heartache.

Health issues

In common with all purebred dogs, the Bulldog suffers from some hereditary problems so you need to talk to the breeder about the health status of breeding stock and find out if there are any issues or concerns. For information on inherited conditions, see page 182.

Puppy watching

Bulldog puppies are totally irresistible, and when you see a litter you will want to take the whole lot home with you! However, you must try to put your feelings to one side so that you can make an informed choice.

You need to be 100 per cent confident that the breeding stock is healthy, and the puppies have been reared with love and care, before making a commitment to buy.

Viewing a litter

It is a good idea to have a mental checklist of what to look out for when you visit a breeder.
You want to see:

- A clean, hygienic environment.

- Puppies who are out-going and friendly, and eager to meet you.

- A sweet natured mother who is ready to show off her babies.

- Puppies that are well covered, but not pot-bellied, which could be an indication of worms.

- Bright eyes, with no sign of soreness or discharge.

- Clean ears that smell fresh.

- No discharge from the nose.

- Clean rear ends – matting could indicate upset tummies.

- Lively pups who are keen to play.

It is important that you see the mother with her puppies, as this will give you a good idea of the temperament they are likely to inherit. It is also helpful if you can see other close relatives so you can see the type of Bulldog the breeder produces.

In most cases, you will not be able to see the father (sire) as most breeders will travel some distance to find a stud dog that is not too close to their own bloodlines and complements their bitch. However, you should be able to see photos of him and be given the chance to examine his pedigree and show record.

Companion puppy

If you are looking for a Bulldog purely as a companion, you should be guided by the breeder who will have spent hours and hours puppy watching, and will know each of the pups as individuals. It is tempting to choose a puppy yourself, but the breeder will take into account your family set up and lifestyle and will help you to pick the most suitable puppy.

Show puppy

If you are buying a puppy with the hope of showing him, make sure you make this clear to the breeder. A lot of planning goes into producing a litter, and although all the puppies will have been reared with equal care, there will be one or two that have show potential.

Ideally, recruit a breed expert to inspect the puppies with you, so you have the benefit of their objective evaluation. The breeder will also be there to help as they will want to ensure that only the best of their stock is exhibited in the show ring. The optimum age to select a show puppy is between seven and eight weeks when he will look like a miniature version of the adult dog. Thereafter, he will go through different phases and may look different from one week to the next before he reaches full maturity.

A puppy with show potential should have a stocky, short-backed body. As already highlighted (see page 32), a roach back, where the rear end is higher that the shoulders, is a feature of the breed. This should be evident in a puppy, but not exaggerated. He should have a well-defined neck and good front and rear angulation.

Within a litter there will be a variety of straight and screwed tails; the length and shape of tail will also

Facing page: The breeder will know the puppies as individuals.

vary. In Britain, straight tails are encouraged but, at the present time, screw tails are not penalised in the show ring. However, straight tails are increasingly becoming the norm, so this situation may well change. Certainly, a tightly screwed tail should be avoided on health grounds.

When looking at a puppy with a straight tail, look for a low set, with a downward carriage. The Bulldog's head is of paramount importance in show dogs, and an expert will be able to assess specific features to judge whether a puppy has the potential to fulfil the very demanding stipulations laid down in the Breed Standard.

You will be looking for:

- A brick-shaped head when viewed from the front and the side.

- The top of the skull should be flat and broad. There should be some wrinkling but it should not be excessive.

- At eight weeks the ears will probably hang forwards, but if they are small and thin, they should develop into the ideal 'rose' shape (see page 31) by the time a puppy is around four months of age.

- The nose and nostrils should be large and black.

- The eyes should be round, dark, set wide apart, and on the same straight line as the stop (the step up between the muzzle and the forehead).

- When you look at the puppy's mouth from straight on, the front under jaw should be directly under the upper jaw.

Remember temperament and health should always be a major consideration, as the time spent showing a dog during his lifetime is very small compared to the time spent living at home as a treasured member of your family circle.

Facing page: It takes an expert eye to assess show potential

A Bulldog friendly home

It may seem an age before your Bulldog puppy is ready to leave the breeder and move to his new home. But you can fill the time by getting your house and garden ready, and buying the equipment you will need.

These preparations apply to a new puppy but, in reality, they are the means of creating an environment that is safe and secure for your Bulldog throughout his life.

In the home

Nothing is safe when a puppy is about – and the Bulldog is certainly no exception. Everything is new and exciting for a young puppy – and it all needs thorough investigation!

Bulldog puppies are generally more chilled out than some of the working breeds, but one thing is certain, a free ranging Bulldog puppy cannot be trusted.

Remember, it is not only your prized possessions that are under threat, equally relevant is the damage a puppy can inflict on himself.

Trailing electric cables are a major hazard so these will need to be secured out of reach. You will need to make sure all cupboards and storage units cannot be opened – or broken into.

This applies particularly in the kitchen, where you may store cleaning materials, and other substances, which could be toxic to dogs. There are a number of household plants that are poisonous, so these will need to relocated, along with breakable ornaments.

A Bulldog puppy is weighty in relation to his size, which means that while he is growing his joints are vulnerable and any mishap could prove to be serious. Most owners find it is easier to make upstairs off-limits right from the start.

The best way of doing this is to use a baby gate; these can also be useful if you want to limit your Bulldog's freedom in any other part of the house.

In the garden

The Bulldog is very much a people dog and he has no plans to escape from the comforts of his home and the companionship of his beloved family. However, it is essential that your garden is fenced to a minimum height of 1.20m (4 ft), and gates must have secure fastenings.

Remember, Bulldogs are valuable animals, and so you also need to guard against any possibility of intruders getting into your garden.

For this reason, you need to be careful about leaving your adult Bulldog unattended in the garden, and vigilance should be considered essential for a puppy.

A Bulldog puppy loves to explore and will squeeze himself out of a gap in the fence, just to see what is on the other side!

He may also take an interest in gardening, which may involve some concentrated digging or maybe sampling some of your plants.

This can be very annoying, especially if you are proud of your garden, but, worse still, it can be positively dangerous.

There are a number of plants which are toxic to dogs, and the consequence of ingesting poisonous plant material could be very serious.

You therefore need to find out which plants might be poisonous and take preventative action before your puppy arrives in his new home.

It could be that you decide to fence off part of

your garden in order to ensure that it is 100 per cent Bulldog friendly.

Swimming pools and ponds should be covered as most puppies are fearless and, although it is easy for a puppy to take the plunge, it is virtually impossible for him to get out – with potentially lethal consequences.

You will also need to designate a toileting area. This will assist the house training process, and it will also make cleaning up easier. For information on house-training, see page 96.

House rules

Before your puppy comes home, hold a family conference to decide on the house rules. You need to decide which rooms your puppy will have access to, and establish whether he is to be allowed on the furniture or not. It is important to start as you mean to go on. You cannot invite a puppy on to the sofa for cuddles only to decide in a few months' time that this is no longer desirable.

The Bulldog likes to please, but he can sometimes follow his own agenda and be a little stubborn if he you try to change his preferred course of action.

However, if house rules are applied consistently, he will understand what is – and what is not – allowed, and he will soon learn to respect you and co-operate.

The inquisitive Bulldog will explore every nook and cranny of his house and garden.

Buying equipment

There are some essential items of equipment you will need for your Bullmastiff. If you choose wisely, much of it will last for many years to come.

Indoor crate

Rearing a puppy is so much easier if you invest in an indoor crate. It provides a safe haven for your puppy at night, when you have to go out during the days, and at other times when you cannot supervise him. A puppy needs a base where he feels safe and secure, and where he can rest undisturbed. An indoor crate provides the perfect den, and many adults continue to use them throughout their lives.

Bearing this in mind, it is sensible to buy a crate that will be big enough for your Bulldog when he is fully grown. The recommended size is 76cm x 51cm x 61cm (30in x 20in x 24in). What starts as a safe place for keeping your puppy when you cannot supervise him soon becomes your dog's preferred resting place. If you leave the crate door open you will find that your adult Bulldog will choose to go in and out of his crate as he chooses. You will also need to consider where you are going to locate the crate. The kitchen is usually the most suitable place as this is the hub of family life. Try to find a snug corner where the puppy can rest when he wants to, but where he can also see what is going on around him, and still be with the family.

Play pen

These are becoming increasingly popular with Bulldog owners, providing a more spacious alternative to a crate; a puppy has room to play but is still safely confined. A puppy should not be left in a playpen if you are going out or if you are elsewhere in the house for an extended period of time.

However, it provides a safe option when you are busy, cleaning the house for example, and you do not want your puppy to get involved. A playpen has the added benefit that it has good visibility so your pup does not feel excluded from the family's activities.

Beds and bedding

The crate will need to be lined with bedding and the best type to buy is synthetic fleece. This is warm and cosy, and as moisture soaks through it, your puppy will not have a wet bed when he is tiny and still unable to go through the night without relieving himself. This type of bedding is machine washable and easy to dry; buy two pieces, so you have one to use while the other piece is in the wash. If you have purchased a crate, you may not feel the need to buy an extra bed, although your Bulldog may like to have a bed in the family room so he feels part of household activities. There is an amazing array of dog-beds to chose from – duvets, bean bags, cushions, baskets, igloos, mini-four posters – so you can take your pick! However, your Bulldog puppy may be destructive while he is teething, so delay making a major investment until he has gone through the worst of the chewing phase.

Collar and lead

You may think that it is not worth buying a collar for the first few weeks, but the sooner your pup gets used to it, the better (see Wearing a Collar, page 136). A soft, leather or nylon collar is recommended as it is lightweight and most puppies will accept it without making a fuss.

When your Bulldog matures, you need to be aware of the size of your Bulldog's neck, making sure the collar is comfortable but not so loose that he can slip it. As sizing can be a problem, many owners opt for a harness, which works well with dogs that have a tendency to pull on the lead. The lead can be leather or nylon, depending on personal preference but check that it has a secure trigger fastening.

Facing page: Wait until your Bulldog is fully grown before buying him a more expensive collar.

ID

Your Bulldog needs to wear some kind of ID when he is out in public places. This can be in the form of a disc, engraved with your contact details, attached to the collar. When your Bulldog is full-grown, you can buy an embroidered collar with your contact details, which eliminates the danger of the disc becoming detached from the collar. You may also wish to consider a permanent form of ID. Increasingly breeders are getting puppies micro-chipped before they go to their new homes.

A microchip is the size of a grain of rice. It is 'injected' under the skin, usually between the shoulder blades, with a special needle.

It has some tiny barbs on it, which dig into the tissue around where it lies, so it does not migrate from that spot. Each chip has its own unique identification number, which can only be read by a special scanner.

That ID number is then registered on a national database with your name and details, so that if ever your dog is lost, he can be taken to any vet or rescue centre where he is scanned and then you are contacted. If your puppy has not been micro-chipped, you can ask your vet to do it, maybe when he goes along for his vaccinations.

Check toys regularly for signs of wear and tear.

Bowls

Your Bulldog will need two bowls; one for food, and one for fresh drinking water, which should always be readily available.

A stainless steel bowl is a good choice for a food bowl as it is tough and hygienic. Plastic bowls may be chewed, and there is a danger that bacteria can collect in the small cracks that may appear. You can opt for a second stainless steel bowl for drinking water, or you may prefer a heavier ceramic bowl which will not be knocked over so easily.

Food

The breeder will let you know what your puppy is eating and should provide a full diet sheet to guide you through the first six months of your puppy's feeding regime – how much they are eating per meal, how many meals per day, when to increase the amounts given per meal and when to reduce the meals per day.

The breeder may provide you with some food when you go and collect your puppy, but it is worth making enquiries in advance about the availability of the brand that is recommended. See Choosing a diet, page 100.

Grooming gear

The Bulldog is a low maintenance breed in terms of coat care but there are a few essentials you will need to buy. These include:

- A soft nylon brush or a grooming mitt (a rubber glove with different sized nodules on either side)

- Nail-clippers: Guillotine style clippers are easiest to use.

- Toothbrush and toothpaste: A normal toothbrush is adequate and there are flavoured canine toothpastes on the market which are acceptable to dogs.

- Unscented wet wipes: These are needed for keeping the face folds clean, and also for cleaning under the tail. These are easily obtained from most pet shops and generally come in a tub which is re-sealable to retain moisture.

- Antiseptic cream for the face folds. This can be specially manufactured for dogs or you can use a nappy-rash cream for infants.

- Medicated ear wipes: These will keep the ears fresh and clean.

- Vaseline: To prevent the nose drying out.

Toys

There is a huge variety of toys to choose from, coming in a range of shapes and sizes and made from different materials. Your objective is not to buy the toy that looks cute or the one you think your Bulldog will love, but to buy toys that are safe. A Bulldog has powerful jaws, even when he is quite small, and he can be very destructive. Plastic toys can be shredded and soft toys can be chewed into little pieces.

If your dog swallows part of a toy, it could cause an obstruction which could have lethal consequences. Avoid soft, plastic toys with squeakers and only offer soft toys if the eyes and nose have been removed. The best toys to go for are hard, rubber kongs (which can be filled with food), and tough, fabric tuggies. They may be more expensive, but safety comes first.

Finding a vet

Before your puppy arrives home, you should register with a vet. Visit some of the vets in your local area, and speak to other pet owners to see who they recommend.

It is so important to find a good vet, almost as essential as finding a good doctor for yourself. You need to find someone you can build up a good rapport with and have complete faith in. Word of mouth is really the best recommendation. When you contact a veterinary practice, find out the following:

The vet will be an important person in your Bulldog's life.

- Does the surgery run an appointment system?

- What are the arrangements for emergency, out of hours cover?

- Do any of the vets in the practice have experience treating Bulldogs?

- What facilities are available at the practice?

If you are satisfied with what your find, and the staff appear to be helpful and friendly, book an appointment for your puppy to have a health check a couple of days after you collect him.

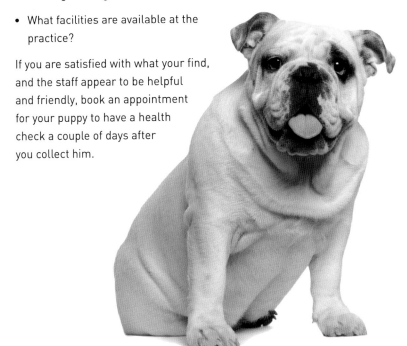

Settling in

When you first arrive home with your puppy, be careful not to overwhelm him. You and your family are hugely excited, but the puppy is in a completely strange environment with new sounds, smells and sights, which is a daunting experience, even for the boldest of pups.

Some puppies are very confident, wanting to play straightaway and quickly making friends; others need a little longer. Keep a close check on your Bulldog's body language and reactions so you can proceed at a pace he is comfortable with. Do not worry if he is a little unsure of himself at first, this will not last long and in no time he will be following you around, watching your every move.

First, let him explore the garden. He will probably need to relieve himself after the journey home, so take him to the allocated toileting area and when he performs give him plenty of praise. When you take your puppy indoors, let him investigate again. Show him his crate, and encourage him to go in by throwing in a treat. Let him have a sniff, and allow him to go in and out as he

wants to. Later on, when he is tired you can put him in the crate while you stay in the room. In this way he will learn to settle and will not think he is being abandoned.

It is a good idea to feed your puppy in his crate, at least to begin with, as this helps to build up a positive association. It will not be long before your Bulldog sees his crate as his own special den and will go there as a matter of choice. Some owners place a blanket over the crate, covering the back and sides, so that it is even more cosy and den-like.

Meeting the family

Resist the temptation of inviting friends and neighbours to come and meet the new arrival; your puppy needs to focus on getting to know his new family for the first few days. Try not to swamp your Bulldog with too much attention; give him a chance to explore and find his feet. There will be plenty of time for cuddles later on!

If you have children in the family, you need to keep everything as calm as possible. Your puppy may not have met children before, and even if he has, he will still find them strange and unpredictable. A puppy can become alarmed by too much noise, or he may go to the opposite extreme and become over-excited, which can lead to mouthing and nipping. The best plan is to get the children to sit on the floor and give them all a

treat. Each child can then call the puppy, stroke him, and offer a treat. In this way the puppy is making the decisions rather than being forced into interactions he may find stressful.

Children should not regard the new puppy as a plaything, so do not leave them unattended with the pup until he has become less of a novelty. You need to supervise play so that neither the children – nor the puppy – become over-excited. Shouting, screaming and running will be highly stimulating, and a puppy will react by chasing, jumping up and maybe scratching by accident. You need to work at establishing calm interactions, ensuring that mutual respect is established.

Below: Bulldogs generally get on well with each other.

A puppy should not be tugged, pinched or teased. If he is eating, he should not be disturbed, and the same applies if his is resting in his bed or in his crate. Never allow a child to pick up a puppy, as it could result in a serious injury or a broken limb if he is dropped.

The resident dog

If you already have an adult dog in the family, you will need to introduce your new puppy tactfully and supervise all their interaction to begin with. The garden is the best place for introducing the puppy, as there is more space and the adult will not feel as though his territory is being invaded. He will probably take a great interest in the puppy and sniff him all over. Most puppies are naturally submissive in this situation; your pup may lick the other dog's mouth or roll over on to his back. Try not to interfere, as this is the natural way that dogs get to know each other. As your Bulldog puppy settles into his new home he will become increasingly confident so you will need to make sure that he does not take too many liberties with the older dog.

Feline friends

A Bulldog does not have a strong prey drive, but the curiosity of a puppy means that a cat is a natural draw. However, harmonious relations can be established if you work at early interactions. You will need to progress step by step, making sure the pair are never left alone together until they have learnt to ignore each other.

Feeding

The breeder will generally provide enough food for the first few days so the puppy does not have to cope with a change in diet – and possible digestive upset – along with all the stress of moving home.

Some puppies polish off their food from the first meal onwards, others are more concerned by their new surroundings and are too distracted to eat. Do not worry unduly if your puppy seems disinterested in his food for the first day or so. Give him 10 minutes to eat what he wants and then remove the leftovers and start afresh at the next meal. Obviously if you have any concerns about your puppy in the first few days, seek advice from your vet.

Bulldogs are not normally possessive over their food, but it is advisable to guard against this tendency from day one. If you have children, you need to establish a rule that no one is to go near the dog when he is feeding. This is sound common sense, and removes all risk of problems arising, no matter how unintentional they may be.

At the same time, you can educate your Bulldog so that he does not become stressed if people are around when he is eating. You can do this by giving him half his ration, and then dropping food around his bowl. This will stop him guarding his bowl and, at the same time, he will see your presence in a positive light. You can also call him away from the bowl and reward him with some food – maybe something extra special – which he can take from your hand. Start doing this as soon as your puppy arrives in his new home, and continue working on it throughout his life. Remember food is a top priority for a dog; he will respect you as the provider and, if you interact with him as described, he will trust you and will not feel threatened.

The first night

Your puppy will have spent the first weeks of his
life with either his mother or curled up with his
siblings. He is then taken from everything he knows
as familiar, lavished with attention by his new family
– and then comes bed time when he is left all alone.
It is little wonder that he feels abandoned. The best
plan is to establish a routine right from the start
so your Bulldog becomes familiar with the ritual of
going to his bed and settling until morning.

Take your puppy out into the garden to relieve
himself, and then encourage him to go into his crate.
You can throw a couple of treats or biscuits in the
crate which will build up a good association with
it, as well as diverting his attention while you close
the door. Some people leave a low light on for the
puppy at night for the first week, others have tried a
radio as company or a ticking clock. A covered hot-
water bottle, filled with warm water, can also be a
comfort. Like people, puppies are all individuals and
what works for one, does not necessarily work for
another, so it is a matter of trial and error.

Be very positive when you leave your puppy on his
own. Do not linger, or keep returning; this will make
the situation more difficult. It is inevitable that he
will protest to begin with, but if you stick to your

routine, he will accept that he gets left at night – but you always return in the morning.

Rescued dogs

Settling an older, rescued dog in the home is very similar to a puppy in as much as you will need to make the same preparations regarding his homecoming. As with a puppy, with an older dog will need you to be consistent, so start as you mean to go on. There is often an initial honeymoon period when you bring a rescued dog home, where he will be on his best behaviour for the first few weeks. It is after these first couple of weeks that the true nature of the dog will show, so be prepared for subtle changes in his behaviour. It may be advisable to register with a reputable training club, so you can seek advice on any training or behavioural issues at an early stage.

Above all, remember that a rescued dog ceases to be a rescued dog the moment he enters his forever home and should be treated like any other family dog.

House training

This is the aspect of training that puppy owners dread – but it doesn't have to be an ordeal if you put in the time and effort in the first few weeks.

The key to successful house training is vigilance and consistency. If you establish a routine, and stick to it, your puppy will understand what is required.

Equally, you must be there to supervise him at all times – except when he is safely tucked up in his crate. It is when a puppy is left to wander from room to room that accidents are most likely to happen.

As discussed earlier, you will have allocated a toileting area in your garden when preparing for your puppy's homecoming.

You must take your puppy to this area every time he needs to relieve himself so he builds up an association and knows why you have brought him out to the garden.

Establish a routine and make sure you take your puppy out at the following times:

- First thing in the morning

- After mealtimes

- On waking from a sleep

- Following a play session

- Last thing at night.

A puppy should be taken out to relieve himself every two hours as an absolute minimum. If you can manage an hourly trip out so much the better. The more often your puppy gets it 'right', the quicker he will learn to be clean in the house. It helps if you use a verbal cue, such as "Busy", when your pup is performing and, in time, this will trigger the desired response.

Do not be tempted to put your puppy out on the doorstep in the hope that he will toilet on his own. Most pups simply sit there, waiting to get back inside the house! No matter how bad the weather is, accompany your puppy and give him lots of praise when he performs correctly.

Do not rush back inside as soon as he has finished, your puppy might start to delay in the hope of prolonging his time outside with you. Praise him, have a quick game – and then you can both return indoors.

When accidents happen

No matter how vigilant you are, there are bound to be accidents. If you witness the accident, take your puppy outside immediately, and give him lots of praise if he finishes his business out there.

If you are not there when he has an accident, do not scold him when you discover what has happened. He will not remember what he has done and will not understand why you are cross with him. Simply clean it up and resolve to be more vigilant next time.

Make sure you use a deodoriser (available in pet stores) when you clean up, otherwise your pup will be drawn to the smell and may be tempted to use the same spot again.

Choosing a diet

There are so many different types of dog food on sale – all claiming to be the best – so how do you know what is likely to suit your Bulldog?

When choosing a diet, there are basically three categories to choose from:

Complete

This is probably the most popular diet as it is easy to feed and is specially formulated with all the nutrients your dog needs. This means that you should not add any supplements or you may upset the nutritional balance.

Most complete diets come in different life stages: puppy, adult maintenance and senior, so this means that your Bulldog is getting what he needs when he is growing, during adulthood, and as he becomes older. You can even get prescription diets for dogs with particular health issues.

When choosing a complete diet, opt for larger size kibble as a Bulldog can 'lose' small size segments from the side of his mouth as he eats. You also need to check protein levels; a low protein diet of around 20 per cent is most suitable for a Bulldog.

Canned / pouches

This type of food is usually fed with hard biscuit, and most Bulldogs find it very appetizing.

However, the ingredients – and the nutritional value – vary significantly between the different brands so you will need to check the label. This type of food often has a high moisture content, so you need to be sure your Bulldog is getting all the nutrition he needs.

Homemade

There are some owners who like to prepare meals especially for their dogs – and it is probably much appreciated.

The danger is that although the food is tasty, and your Bulldog may appreciate the variety, you cannot be sure that it has the correct nutritional balance.

If this is a route you want to go down, you will need to find out the exact ratio of fats, carbohydrates, proteins, minerals and vitamins that are needed, which is quite an undertaking. The Barf (Biologically

Appropriate Raw Food) diet is another, more natural approach to feeding. Dogs are fed a diet mimicking what they would have eaten in the wild, consisting of raw meat, bone, muscle, fat, and vegetable matter. If you choose this diet it will need to be modified. Bulldogs have a tendency to swallow chicken wings whole, which could result in choking. The best plan is to substitute this part of the diet with minced chicken.

The breeder will give you valuable advice on the best nutrition for your Bulldog.

Feeding regime

Most pups at eight weeks are on three or four meals a day, depending on the appetite of the individual, and it is sensible to stick to the diet recommended by the breeder for the initial few weeks to avoid the risk of stomach upset.

When your puppy has settled, you may wish to change to a different type of complete feed – some are more easily available than others. Having said this, never feed a puppy on what is easiest for you – quality should never be sacrificed for convenience. Generally speaking, the protein content in most complete puppy food ranges from 27 to 34 per cent for the large/giant breeds.

The Bulldog is not the greediest feeder and you may find you have to tempt your pup a little when he first leaves the nest and does not have the competition of his siblings around him.

A small amount of chicken or cheese sprinkled on his complete, should be enough to tempt your puppy's appetite. When your puppy is around 12 weeks, you can cut out one of his meals; he may well have started to leave some of his food, indicating he is ready to do this.

By six months, he can move on to two meals a day – a regime that will suit him for the rest of his life.

Some Bulldogs seem to struggle with two meals so, if this is the case, he may do better with a single meal. All dogs are individuals so monitor your dog and work out what suits him best.

A dog should not be fed prior to exercise, or immediately afterwards as this can result in a potentially lethal condition known as bloat. Make sure you leave a minimum period of an hour, either side of mealtimes, before exercising your Bulldog.

Faddy feeders

Bulldogs are not always the most enthusiastic feeders, and it is tempting to try to entice your dog to eat. One look from those dark eyes is enough to melt your heart, stirring you to greater efforts to find a food that he will really like.

At first you may add some gravy, then you may try some chicken... The clever Bulldog will quickly realize that if he holds out, tastier treats will follow.

If your dog is turning up his nose at mealtimes, give him 10 minutes to eat what he wants, and then take up his bowl and give him fresh food at his next mealtime.

Do not feed him treats in between meals. If you continue this regime for a couple of days, your Bulldog will realise that there is no percentage in holding out for better food as it never materialises. In most cases, this is just a 'trying it on' phase, and if you cope with common sense, you will soon return to the status quo and your Bulldog will be content with his normal rations.

If, however, your dog refuses all food for more than 24 hours you need to observe his behaviour to see if there are any signs of ill health, which may indicate a need for a veterinary check up.

Bones and chews

Puppies love to chew, and many adults also enjoy gnawing on a bone. Bones should always be hard and uncooked; rib bones and poultry bones must be avoided as they can splinter and cause major problems.

Dental chews, and some of the manufactured rawhide chews are safe, but they should only be given under supervision.

Ideal weight

With his relatively short legs and powerfully built body, it is not always easy to detect when your Bulldog is putting on weight, and with a breed that does not believe in strenuous exercise, it is all too easy to give your dog more food than he needs.

Obesity is a major problem in Bulldogs, and this can have devastating effects not only on your dog's quality of life but also on his longevity. An overweight dog will become lethargic and will cease to engage in family activities because it is all too much effort.

His health will also be affected; overweight dogs are prone to heart conditions, diabetes, joint problems and digestive disorders. Your dog's life expectancy will be seriously threatened if he is moderately obese.

When judging your Bulldog's condition, look at him from above, and make sure you can see a definite 'waist'. You should be able to feel his ribs, but not see them.

If you are concerned about your Bulldog's weight, get into the habit of visiting your veterinary surgery on a monthly basis so that you can weigh him. You can keep a record of his weight so you can make adjustments if necessary.

Facing page: You need to monitor your Bulldog's weight throughout his life.

Caring for your bulldog

The shorthaired Bulldog is low maintenance in terms of coat care, but like all breeds he has his own special needs which you must take on board.

Puppy care

When your Bulldog puppy first arrives in his new home at around eight weeks of age, he will need little in the way of coat care, but it is essential that he gets used to being handled. Throughout his life he will need to be groomed, undergo routine preventative health care, and on occasion, he will need to be examined by a vet. If he is accustomed to handling from an early age, the stress you both experience will be minimal

Start by handling your puppy all over, stroking him from his head to his tail. Lift up each paw in turn, and reward him with a treat when he co-operates. Then roll him over on to his back and tickle his tummy; this is a very vulnerable position for a dog to adopt, so do not force the issue. Be firm but gentle, and give your puppy lots of praise when he does as you ask.

Adult grooming

The Bulldog's short, smooth coat requires the minimum of grooming, but not do neglect this area of care. Remember that as well as keeping the coat in good order, grooming acts as a massage and aids circulation. It also gives you the opportunity to check your Bulldog to discover if he has any sore places or unusual lumps or bumps.

Problems spotted at an early stage are always easier to treat. Spend a few minutes brushing the coat every day, using a soft body brush. If you want your dog's coat to shine, you can give him a wipe over with a piece of silk.

Some Bulldog owners also use a spray-on conditioner to keep the coat at its best. Bulldogs do shed their coats; in centrally heated houses this tends to be an on-going process rather than a seasonal moult. However, if you feel your Bulldog is shedding more than normal, you can use a stripping blade which helps to get rid of the dead hair.

Routine care

As well as looking after your Bulldog's coat, you need to adopt a regime of routine care which will keep him healthy and will prevent problems arising.

Facial care

The Bulldog's wrinkles are a characteristic of the breed – they make a Bulldog look like a Bulldog. Modern breeders steer clear of exaggeration, and so this feature should not be overdone, but even modest wrinkling needs daily attention. If the skin between the wrinkles becomes moist, soreness and infection can easily develop.

You therefore need to use unscented wipes to clean the skin, dry with cotton-wool and then apply an antiseptic powder. If the skin looks red or inflamed, you should apply a nappy-rash cream.

Eyes

Your Bulldog's eyes should appear bright, clear and clean. You can purchase proprietary brands of eye wipes that can be used to clean 'sleep' discharge which can be present in the morning. Some Bulldogs are prone to tear-staining; if this is the case with your Bulldog, use unscented wipes to clean the face. Staining can be kept to a minimum if you apply a small pinch of Boric powder, which you can buy at a pharmacy. If your Bulldog's eyes look red or inflamed, or if there is evidence of discharge, you should make an appointment with the vet without delay.

Ears

At your regular grooming session, inspect your Bulldog's ears to make sure they are clean and free from odour. There are several safe proprietary brands of ear cleaner that can be bought from a pet shop but if you notice your Bulldog scratching his ears, shaking his head or holding his head to one side, then a visit to the vet may be necessary to obtain specific medication.

Grooming provides an opportunity to give your Bulldog a thorough check-up.

Nail trimming does not need to be a battle!

Folds on the face need to be be kept clean and dry.

Tail

The Bulldog's tail is naturally undocked, varies in size and length, and may be straight or screwed.

Keep a close check on the tail area to ensure it is clean and free from hair which could be an irritation. If the tail is clamped tight to the anus – now considered a fault in the breed – use nappy rash cream to prevent problems arising.

Teeth

Dental disease is increasing among dogs so teeth cleaning should be seen as an essential part of your care regime.

The build up of tartar on the teeth can result in tooth decay, gum infection and bad breath, and if it is allowed to accumulate, you may have no option but to get the teeth cleaned under anaesthetic.

When your Bulldog is still a puppy, accustom him to teeth cleaning so it becomes a matter of routine.

Dog toothpaste comes in a variety of meaty flavours, which your Bulldog will like, so you can start by putting toothpaste on your finger and gently rubbing his teeth.

You can then progress to using a finger brush or a toothbrush, whichever you find most convenient.

Remember to reward your Bulldog when he co-operates and then he will positively look forward to his teeth-cleaning sessions.

Nails

Nail trimming is a task dreaded by many owners – and many dogs – but, again, if you start early on, your Bulldog will get used to the task you have to perform and will not fight against it.

Depending on his colour, your Bulldog may have white or black nails. In a white nail you can see the quick, the vein that runs through the nail, but this is obscured in black nails.

For this reason, you should only trim the tips of the nails so you don't cut into the quick. If you do this inadvertently, it is not disastrous, but it will cause the nail to bleed profusely.

This will be uncomfortable for your Bulldog and he will remember it next time you attempt to trim his nails.

If you are worried about trimming your Bulldog's nails, go to your vet so you can see it done properly.

If you are still concerned, you can always use the services of a professional groomer.

Exercise

The Bulldog enjoys going out and about; he relishes the opportunity to use his nose and loves to be stimulated by new surroundings. He does not need the exercise required by working and sporting breeds, but do not neglect this aspect of his care. A fit Bulldog will, undoubtedly, lead a longer, healthier life. The Bulldog is a heavy dog for his size, so you need to limit exercise during the vulnerable growing period.

Time out in the garden, short lead-walking expeditions for socialisation, and 10 minute off-lead sessions should be considered sufficient for the first 12 months. Bulldogs that are over-exercised while they are growing can damage their joints and they also risk bone distortion. The adult Bulldog will appreciate daily outings, and the more variety you can provide, the better. Most Bulldogs have a burst of activity – particularly young, adolescent dogs – and then take things at their own pace. Some enjoy retrieve games or playing hide-and-seek which provides mental stimulation as well as physical exercise.

The older Bulldog

The Bulldog is not the most long-lived of breeds – the average life expectancy is 8 to 10 years - so

you need to take the greatest care of him when he starts to age. The timing of this will vary from dog to dog but there is no doubt that a fit dog, kept at the correct weight, will have an enhanced life expectancy. The older Bulldog may sleep more and may be reluctant to go for longer walks. He may show signs of stiffness when he gets up from his bed, but these generally ease when he starts moving. Some older Bulldogs may have impaired vision, and some become a little deaf, but as long as their senses do not deteriorate dramatically, this is something older dogs learn to live with.

If you treat your older dog with kindness and consideration, he will enjoy his later years and suffer the minimum of discomfort. It is advisable to switch him over to a senior diet, which is more suited to his needs, and you may need to adjust the quantity, as he will not be burning up the calories as he did when he was younger and more energetic.

Make sure his sleeping quarters are warm and free from draughts, and if he gets wet, make sure you dry him thoroughly. Most important of all, be guided by your Bulldog. He will have good days when he feels up to going for a walk, and other days when he would prefer to potter in the garden.

If you have a younger dog at home, this may stimulate your Bulldog to take more of an interest in what is going on, but make sure he is not pestered, as he needs to rest undisturbed when he is tired.

Letting go

Inevitably there comes a time when your Bulldog is not enjoying a good quality of life, and you need to make the painful decision to let him go. We would all wish that our dogs died, painlessly, in their sleep but, unfortunately, this is rarely the case. However, we can allow our dogs to die with dignity, and to suffer as a little as possible, and this should be our way of saying thank you for the wonderful companionship they have given us.

When you feel the time is drawing close, talk to your vet who will be able to make an objective assessment of your Bulldog's condition and will help you to make the right decision.

This is the hardest thing you will ever have to do as a dog owner, and it is only natural to grieve for your beloved Bulldog. But eventually, you will be able to look back on the happy memories of times spent together, and this will bring much comfort. You may, in time, realise that your life is not complete without a Bulldog, and will feel ready to welcome a new puppy into your home

Social skills

To live in the modern world, without fears and anxieties, your Bulldog needs to receive an education in social skills so that he learns to cope calmly and confidently in a wide variety of situations.

The Bulldog is a naturally sociable and out-going dog, but you need to maximise learning opportunities, particularly in the first 12 months of his life.

Early learning

The breeder will have begun a programme of socialisation by getting the puppies used to all the sights and sounds of a busy household. You need to continue this when your pup arrives in his new home, making sure he is not worried by household equipment, such as the vacuum cleaner or the washing machine, and that he gets used to unexpected noises from the radio and television.

To begin with, your puppy needs to get used to all the members of his new family (see Meeting the Family, page 88), but then you should give him the opportunity to meet other people that come to the house. If you do not have children of your own, make sure your puppy has the chance to meet and play with other people's children – making sure interactions are always supervised – so he learns that humans come in small sizes, too.

The outside world

When your puppy has completed his vaccinations, he is ready to venture into the outside world. As a breed, the Bulldog is pretty laid back but there is a lot for a youngster to take on board, so do not swamp him with too many new experiences when you first set out.

Obviously you need to work at lead-training (see page 138) before your first expedition. There will be plenty of distractions, so you do not want additional problems of coping with a dog that is pulling or lagging on the lead.

So, hopefully, you can set off with your Bulldog walking by your side on a loose lead. He may need additional encouragement when you venture further afield, so arm yourself with some extra special treats, which will give him a good reason to focus on you when required!

Start socialising your puppy in a quiet area with light traffic, and only progress to a busier place when he is ready. There is so much to see and hear – people (maybe carrying bags or umbrellas), pushchairs, bicycles, cars, lorries, machinery – so give your puppy a chance to take it all in.

If he does appear worried, do not fall into the trap of sympathising with him, or worse still, picking him up. This will only teach your pup that he had a good reason to be worried and, with luck, you will 'rescue' him if he feels scared.

Instead, give a little space so he does not have to confront whatever he is frightened of, and distract him with a few treats. Then encourage him to walk past, using an encouraging tone of voice, never forcing him by yanking on the lead. Reward him for any forward movement, and your puppy will soon learn that he can trust you, and there is nothing to fear.

Dog to dog meetings

Your pup also needs to continue his education in canine manners, started by his mother and by his littermates, as he needs to be able to greet all dogs calmly, giving the signals that say he is friendly and offers no threat.

This is especially important with a Bulldog as his unique appearance can be the cause of his downfall.

Dogs use body language and facial expressions to communicate with each other and most breeds struggle to read what is going on with the Bulldog.

His large head, massive, undershot jaw, and wrinkles give him a particular 'look' which we humans love, but can be baffling to other dogs.

Added to this, the Bulldog's shape, and lack of tail, means that signalling through body language is necessarily limited.

If a dog is unsure, or even fearful when meeting a Bulldog, he may become assertive simply because he doesn't know what else to do.

A Bulldog may well start off with good intentions, but if he senses the other's dog's uncertainty and suspicion, he may become reactive.

The Bulldog's fighting instincts, born from his ancestry as a bull-baiting dog, are hugely diluted, but if he feels threatened, he will look after himself – and this could be problematical.

Therefore it is important that your Bulldog learns to give off good vibes, greeting dogs calmly and quietly so they have nothing to worry about.

Facing page: A puppy needs to continue the social education which was started by his mother and his littermates.

Try the following:
Find a friend who has a dog with a bombproof temperament and visit their house. Allow the two dogs to play in the garden for 10 minutes or so. Do not prolong the game, as you do not want your youngster to become over-excited, or overwhelmed.

Once the two dogs have had a few play-dates at home, go for a walk and allow them to exercise together off lead. They will interact with each other, but their focus will shift periodically as they become distracted by other sights and smells.

Now extend your Bulldog's circle of acquaintance by finding other friends who have dogs of sound temperament. The more your Bulldog practises meeting and greeting the better he will become at reading body language and assessing other dogs' intentions.

Training classes

A training class will give your Bulldog the opportunity to work alongside other dogs in a controlled situation, and he will also learn to focus on you in a different, distracting environment. Both these lessons will be vital as your dog matures.

However, the training class needs to be of the highest calibre or you risk doing more harm than

Socialise your Bulldog with dogs of proven, sound temperament.

good. Before you go along with your puppy, attend a class as an observer to make sure you are happy with what goes on. Find out the following:

- How much training experience do the instructors have?

- Are the classes divided into appropriate age categories?

- Do they use positive, reward-based training methods?

- Do any of the instructors have experience with Bulldogs?

If the training class is well run, it is certainly worth attending. Both you and your Bulldog will learn useful training exercises.

It will increase his social skills, and you will have the chance to talk to lots of like-minded dog enthusiasts.

Facing page:The Bulldog is a calm, self-assured dog who will learn to take all situations in his stride.

Training guidelines

The Bulldog is a thinking dog and, while there is no doubting his intelligence, he may be reluctant to co-operate if he doesn't see the point in what you are asking him to do. It is therefore important to keep training sessions both short and positive, with lots of rewards to keep him fully motivated.

You will be keen to get started but in your rush to get training underway, do not neglect the fundamentals that could make the difference between success and failure.

You need to get into the mindset of a Bullldog, working out what makes him tick and, equally, what makes him switch off. Decide on your priorities for training, set realistic targets, and then think of ways of making your training as effective, and as fun, as possible.

When you start training, try to observe the following guidelines:

Choose an area that is free from distractions so your puppy will focus on you. You can progress to a more challenging environment as your pup progresses.

Do not train your puppy just after he has eaten or when you have returned from exercise. He will either be too full, or too tired, to concentrate.

Do not train if you are in a bad mood, or if you are short of time – these sessions always end in disaster!

Providing a worthwhile reward is an essential tool in training. You will probably get the best results if you use some extra special food treats, such as cheese or cooked liver.

Some Bulldogs will work for a toy, but they are the exception rather than the rule.

If you decide to use a toy, make sure it is only brought out for training sessions so that it accrues added value.

Keep your verbal cues simple, and always use the same one for each exercise. For example, when you ask your puppy to go into the Down position, the cue is "Down", not "Lie Down", Get Down", or anything else.

Remember, your Bulldog does not speak English; he

associates the sound of the word with the action.

If your dog is finding an exercise difficult, break it down into small steps so it is easier to understand. The Bulldog can be stubborn, and if he becomes frustrated he may decide on a 'down tools' policy.

Do not make your training sessions boring and repetitious. Your Bulldog will be quick to lose interest if there are no tangible rewards on offer.

Do not train for too long, particularly with a young puppy that has a very short attention span, and always end training sessions on a positive note.

This does not necessarily mean getting an exercise right. If your pup is tired and making mistakes, ask him to do a simple exercise so you have the opportunity to praise and reward him.

You may well find that he benefits from having a break and will make better progress next time you try.

Remember that if your Bulldog is rewarded for a behaviour, he is likely to repeat it – so make sure you are 100 per cent consistent and always reward the 'right' behaviour.

First lessons

Like all puppies, a young Bulldog will soak up new experiences like a sponge, so training should start from the time your pup arrives in his new home.

Wearing a collar

You may, or may not, want your Bulldog to wear a collar all the time. But when he goes out in public places he will need to be on a lead, and so he should be used to the feel of a collar around his neck. The best plan is to accustom your pup to wearing a soft collar for a few minutes at a time until he gets used to it.

Fit the collar so that you can get at least two fingers between the collar and his neck. Then have a game to distract his attention. This will work for a few moments; then he will stop, put his back leg up behind his neck and scratch away at the peculiar itchy thing round his neck, which feels so odd.

Bend down, rotate the collar, pat him on the head and distract him by playing with a toy or giving him a treat. Once he has worn the collar for a few minutes each day, he will soon ignore it and become used to it.

Remember, never leave the collar on the puppy unsupervised, especially when he is outside in the garden, or when he is in his crate, as it is could get snagged, causing serious injury.

Walking on the lead

This is a simple exercise, but the Bulldog can be a little stubborn, so it is a good idea to master the basics at home before venturing into the outside world where there is so much to distract him.

Once your puppy is used to the collar, take him outside into your secure garden where there are no distractions. Attach the lead and, to begin with, allow him to wander with the lead trailing, making sure it does not become snagged.

Then pick up the lead and follow the pup where he wants to go; he needs to get used to the sensation of being attached to you.

The next stage is to get your Bulldog to follow you, and for this you will need some treats. To give yourself the best chance of success, make sure the treats are high value – cheese, sausage or cooked liver – so your Bulldog is motivated to work with you.

Show him you have a treat in your hand, and then encourage him to follow you. Walk a few paces, and if he is walking with you, stop and reward him. If he puts on the brakes, simply change direction and lure him with the treat.

Next introduce some changes of direction so your puppy is walking confidently alongside you. At this stage, introduce a verbal cue "Heel" when your puppy is in the correct position.

You can then graduate to walking your puppy outside the home – as long as he has completed his vaccination programme – starting in quiet areas and building up to busier environments.

Training strategy

The Bulldog is a strong, muscular dog and any tendency to pull on the lead should be discouraged. It is unpleasant for you, and puts pressure on your dog's respiratory system as he strains against you. Your dog needs to learn, right from the start, that there is absolutely no percentage in pulling.

Restrict lead training to the garden in the initial stages so you are working in an environment that is free from distractions.

Walk a few paces, being very aware of any tension on the lead. If you feel the lead tighten and your Bulldog is attempting to get ahead of you, stop, change direction, and set off again.

Your Bulldog needs to understand that pulling ahead has exactly the opposite effect to that which he wants. Rather than calling the shots, he has to co-operate with you.

Keep a good supply of tasty treats and remember only reward – with food and with verbal praise – when he is walking on a loose lead by your side.

The mistake made by many owners at this stage is to use the treats to lure the dog into position rather than rewarding him for the correct behaviour.

Keep training sessions short, and when you are ready to venture into the outside world, do not be too ambitious to begin with. Build up the level of distraction and the duration of lead walking only when your Bulldog is consistently showing the behaviour you want.

Facing page: Your Bulldog will grow into a powerful animal so lead walking manners are essential

Come when called

The Bulldog is utterly devoted to his family, but there are times when he gets distracted. There are so many enticing smells out there, you can appreciate that an instant response to the recall may not always be his preferred option.

The key to successful recall training is to start early, and to teach your Bulldog to focus on you, regardless of temptations...

Hopefully, the breeder will have laid the foundations simply by calling the puppies to "Come" when it is dinnertime, or when they are moving from one place to another.

You can build on this when your puppy arrives in his new home, calling him to "Come" when he is in a confined space, such as the kitchen. This is a good place to build up a positive association with the verbal cue – particularly if you ask your puppy to "Come" to get his dinner!

The next stage is to transfer the lesson to the garden. Arm yourself with some treats, and wait until your puppy is distracted. Then call him, using a higher-pitched, excited tone of voice. At this stage, a puppy wants to be with you, so capitalize on this and keep practising the verbal cue, and rewarding your puppy with a treat and lots of praise when he comes to you.

Now you are ready to introduce some distractions. Try calling him when someone else is in the garden, or wait a few minutes until he is investigating a really interesting scent.

When he responds, make a really big fuss of him and give him some extra treats so he knows it is worth his while to come to you. If your puppy responds, immediately reward him with a treat.

If he is slow to come, run away a few steps and then call again, making yourself sound really exciting. Jump up and down, open your arms wide to welcome him; it doesn't matter how silly you look, he needs to see you as the most fun person in the world.

When you have a reliable recall in the garden, you can venture into the outside world. Do not be too ambitious to begin with; try a recall on a quiet place with the minimum of distractions so you can be assured of success

Do not make the mistake of only asking your dog to come at the end of his allotted exercise period. What is the incentive in coming back to you if all you do is clip on his lead, marking the end of his free time?

Instead, call your dog at random times, giving him a treat and a stroke, and then letting him go free again. In this way, coming to you – and focusing on you – is always rewarding.

Stationary exercises

The Sit and Down are easy to teach, and mastering these exercises will be rewarding for both you and your Bulldog. They are useful in a wide variety of situations and ensure that you always have a measure of control.

Sit

The best method is to lure your Bulldog into position, and for this you can use a treat or his food bowl.

Hold the reward (a treat or food bowl) above his head. As he looks up, he will lower his hindquarters and go into a sit.

Practise this a few times and when your puppy understands what you are asking, introduce the verbal cue, "Sit".

When your Bulldog understands the exercise, he will respond to the verbal cue alone, and you will not

need to reward him every time he sits. However, it is a good idea to give him a treat on a random basis when he co-operates to keep him guessing!

Down

This is an important lesson, and can be a lifesaver if an emergency arises and you need to bring your Bulldog to an instant halt.

You can start with your dog in a Sit or a Stand for this exercise. Stand or kneel in front of him and show him you have a treat in your hand. Hold the treat just in front of his nose and slowly lower it towards the ground, between his front legs.

As your Bulldog follows the treat he will go down on his front legs and, in a few moments, his hindquarters will follow.

Close your hand over the treat so he doesn't cheat and get the treat before he is in the correct position. As soon as he is in the Down, give him the treat and lots of praise.

Keep practising, and when your Bulldog understands what you want, introduce the verbal cue "Down".

The Down exercise is a useful lesson in self-control.

Control exercises

These exercises are not the most exciting, but they are important in establishing a relationship of mutual respect with your Bulldog.

Wait

This exercise teaches your Bulldog to "Wait" in position until you give the next command. It differs from the Stay exercise, where he must stay where you have left him for a more prolonged period. The most useful application of "Wait" is when you are getting your dog out of the car and you need him to stay in position until you clip on his lead.

Start with your puppy on the lead to give you a greater chance of success. Ask him to "Sit" then stand in front him. Step back one pace, holding your hand, palm flat, facing him. Wait a second and then come back to stand in front of him. You can then reward him and release him with a word, such as "OK".

Practise this a few times, waiting a little longer before you reward him, and then introduce the verbal cue "Wait". You can reinforce the lesson by using it in different situations, such as asking your Bulldog to "Wait" before you put his food bowl down.

Stay

You need to differentiate this exercise from the Wait by using a different hand signal and a different verbal cue.

Start with your Bulldog in the Down, as he is most likely to be secure in this position. Stand by his side and then step forwards, with your hand held back, palm facing the dog.

Step back, release him, and then reward him. Practise until your Bulldog understands the exercise and then introduce the verbal cue "Stay".

Gradually increase the distance you can leave your puppy, and increase the challenge by walking around him – and even stepping over him – so that he learns he must "Stay" until you release him.

Leave

A response to this verbal cue means that your Bulldog will learn to give up a toy on request, and it follows that he will give up anything when he is asked, which is very useful if he has got hold of a forbidden object. This not simply a matter of obeying the verbal cue to "Leave"; it is establishing the status quo where you are the decision-maker and your Bulldog is ready to co-operate with you. Bulldogs have a tendency to guard resources they see as being valuable; this can relate to food, toys, or a comfortable sofa or bed. You therefore need to teach your Bulldog to give up the thing he values without forcing the issue and provoking conflict.

The "Leave" command can be taught quite easily when you are first playing with your puppy. As you gently take a toy from his mouth, introduce the verbal cue, "Leave", and then praise him.

If he is reluctant, swap the toy for another toy or a treat. This will usually do the trick.

Do not try to pull the toy from his mouth if he refuses to give it up, as you will make the situation confrontational. Let the toy go 'dead' in your hand, and then swap it for a new toy, or a really high-value treat so this becomes the better option.

Remember to make a big fuss of your Bulldog when he does as you ask so that he learns that co-operation is always the best – and most rewarding – option.

Opportunities for Bulldogs

The Bulldog is an outstanding companion dog – and he sees this as his main career. He is not ambitious in terms of competing in sporting activities, but if you are prepared to take it steady and have reasonable expectations, he may surprise you!

Good citizen scheme

The Kennel Club Good Citizen Scheme was introduced to promote responsible dog ownership, and to teach dogs basic good manners.

In the US there is one test; in the UK there are four award levels: Puppy Foundation, Bronze, Silver and Gold.

Exercises within the scheme include:

- Walking on lead
- Road walking
- Control at door/gate.
- Food manners
- Recall
- Stay
- Send to bed
- Emergency stop.

Obedience

If your Bulldog masters basic obedience, you may want to get involved in competitive obedience.

The exercises include: heelwork at varying paces with dog and handler following a pattern decided by the judge, stays, recalls, retrieves, sendaways, scent discrimination and distance control.

The exercises get progressively harder as you progress up the classes.

With patience and lots of rewards, a Bulldog will learn the exercises that are used in obedience competitions.

However this is a discipline that calls for a very high degree of precision and accuracy which does not suit all dogs, or all handlers.

Rally O

If you do not want to get involved in the rigours of Competitive Obedience, you may find that a sport called Rally O is more to your liking.

This is loosely based on Obedience, and also has a few exercises borrowed from agility when you get to the highest levels.

Handler and dog must complete a course, in the designated order, which has a variety of different exercises which could number from 12 to 20.

The course is timed and the team must complete within the time limit that is set, but there are no bonus marks for speed.

The great advantage of Rally O is that it is very relaxed, and anyone can compete; indeed, it has proved very popular for handlers with disabilities, as they are able to work their dogs to a high standard and compete on equal terms with other competitors.

Agility

This is not a natural sport for a Bulldog as he does not have the conformation to run at speed around an agility course, negotiating all the equipment.

However, he can have a go at fun agility, jumping at a low height, and going through tunnels, which is enjoyable for both you and your dog. Training clubs often run fun agility classes, and you should consider joining. It's a great way for you and your dog to stay fit.

Showing

Exhibiting a dog in the show ring sounds easy but, in fact, it entails a lot of training and preparation, particularly when you are asking a strong-minded, heavyweight breed to compete in a 'beauty' competition.

Your Bulldog will have to be calm and confident in the busy show atmosphere, so you need to work on his socialisation, and also take him to ringcraft classes so you both learn what is required in the ring.

Your Bulldog will be subjected to a detailed 'hands on' examination by the judge; he must learn to stand still in a show pose and to move on a loose lead so the judge can assess his gait.

Showing at the top level is highly addictive, so watch out, once you start, you will never have a free date in your diary!

The Bulldog is a great crowd-pleaser and will enjoy showing off tricks to family and friends.

|Health care

Your Bulldog is dependent on you for all his needs – food, shelter, and health care. Keeping your dog healthy is not just about taking him to the vet when he is unwell, it is about putting a programme of preventative health care in place, which should start from the moment your puppy, or older dog, arrives in his new home.

Vaccinations

Dogs are subject to a number of contagious diseases. In the old days, these were killers, and resulted in heartbreak for many owners.

Vaccinations have now been developed, and the occurrence of the major infectious diseases is now very rare. However, this will only remain the case if all pet owners follow a strict policy of vaccinating their dogs.

There are vaccinations available for the following diseases:

Adenovirus: (Canine Adenovirus): This affects the liver; affected dogs have a classic 'blue eye'.

Distemper: A viral disease which causes chest and gastro-intestinal damage. The brain may also be affected, leading to fits and paralysis.

Parvovirus: Causes severe gastro enteritis, and most commonly affects puppies.

Leptospirosis: This bacterial disease is carried by rats and affects many mammals, including humans. It causes liver and kidney damage.

Rabies: A virus that affects the nervous system and is invariably fatal. The first signs are abnormal behaviour when the infected dog may bite another animal or a person. Paralysis and death follow. Vaccination is compulsory in most countries. In the UK, dogs travelling overseas must be vaccinated.

Kennel Cough: There are several strains of Kennel Cough, but they all result in a harsh, dry, cough. This disease is rarely fatal; in fact most dogs make a good recovery within a matter of weeks and show few signs of ill health while they are affected. However, kennel cough is highly infectious among dogs that live together so, for this reason, most boarding kennels will insist that your dog is protected by the vaccine, which is given as nose drops.

Lyme Disease: This is a bacterial disease transmitted by ticks (see page 168). The first signs are limping, but the heart, kidneys and nervous system can also be affected. The ticks that transmit the disease occur in specific regions, such as the north-east states of the USA, some of the southern states, California and the upper Mississippi region. Lyme disease is still rare in the UK so vaccinations are not routinely offered.

Vaccination programme

In the USA, the American Animal Hospital Association advises vaccination for core diseases, which they list as: distemper, adenovirus, parvovirus and rabies.

Below: Seek advice as to when to start your puppy's vaccination programme.

The requirement for vaccinating for non-core diseases – leptospirosis, Lyme disease and kennel cough – should be assessed depending on a dog's individual risk and his likely exposure to the disease. In the UK, vaccinations are routinely given for distemper, adenovirus, leptospirosis and parvovirus.

In most cases, a puppy will start his vaccinations at around eight weeks of age, with the second part given a fortnight later. However, this does vary depending on the individual policy of veterinary practices, and the incidence of disease in your area. You should also talk to your vet about whether to give annual booster vaccinations. This depends on an individual dog's levels of immunity, and how long a particular vaccine remains effective.

Parasites

No matter how well you look after your Bulldog, you will have to accept that parasites – internal and external – are ever present, and you need to take preventative action.

Internal parasites: As the name suggests, these parasites live inside your dog. Most will find a home in the digestive tract, but there is also a parasite that lives in the heart. If infestation is unchecked, a dog's health will be severely jeopardised, but routine preventative treatment is simple and effective.

External parasites: These parasites live on your dog's body – in his skin and fur, and sometimes in his ears.

Roundworm

This is found in the small intestine, and signs of infestation will be a poor coat, a pot belly, diarrhoea and lethargy. Pregnant mothers should be treated, but it is almost inevitable that parasites will be passed on to the puppies. For this reason, a breeder will start a worming programme, which you will need to continue. Ask your vet for advice on treatment, which will be required to continue throughout your dog's life.

Tapeworm

Infection occurs when fleas and lice are ingested; the adult worm takes up residence in the small intestine, releasing mobile segments (which contain eggs). These can be seen in a dog's faeces as small rice-like grains. The only other obvious sign of infestation is irritation of the anus. Again, routine preventative treatment is required throughout your Bulldog's life.

Heartworm

This parasite is transmitted by mosquitoes, and so will only occur where these insects thrive. A warm environment is needed for the parasite to develop, so it is more likely to be present in areas with a warm, humid climate. However, it is found in all parts of the USA, although its prevalence does vary. At present, heartworm is rarely seen in the UK. Heartworm live in the right side of the heart. Larvae can grow up to 14 in (35.5 cm) in length. A dog with heartworm is at severe risk from heart failure, so preventative treatment, as advised by your vet, is essential. Dogs living in the USA should have regular blood tests to check for the presence of infection.

Lungworm

Lungworm, or *Angiostrongylus vasorum*, is a parasite that lives in the heart and major blood vessels supplying the lungs. It can cause many problems, such as breathing difficulties, blood-clotting, sickness and diarrhoea, seizures, and can even be fatal. The parasite is carried by slugs and snails, and the dog becomes infected when ingesting these, often accidentally when rummaging through undergrowth. Lungworm is not common, but it is on the increase and a responsible owner should be aware of it. Fortunately, it is easily preventable and even affected dogs usually make a full recovery if treated early enough. Your vet will be able to advise you on the risks in your area and what form of treatment may be required.

Fleas

A dog may carry dog fleas, cat fleas, and even human fleas. The flea stays on the dog only long enough to have a blood meal and to breed, but its presence will result in itching and scratching. If your dog has an allergy to fleas – which is usually a reaction to the flea's saliva – he will scratch himself until he is raw. Spot-on treatment, which should be administered on a routine basis, is easy to use and highly effective on all types of fleas. You can also treat your dog with a spray or with insecticidal shampoo. Bear in mind that the whole environment your dog lives in will need to be sprayed, and all other pets living in your home will also need to be treated.

How to detect fleas

Run a fine comb through your dog's coat, and see if you can detect the presence of fleas on the skin, or clinging to the comb. Alternatively, sit your dog on some white paper and rub his back. This will dislodge faeces from the fleas, which will be visible as small brown specks. To double check, shake the specks on to some damp cotton-wool. Flea faeces consists of the dried blood taken from the host, so if the specks turn a lighter shade of red, you know your dog has fleas.

Ticks

These are blood-sucking parasites which are most frequently found in rural area where sheep or deer are present.

The main danger is their ability to pass Lyme disease to both dogs and humans. Lyme disease is prevalent in some areas of the USA (see page 163), although it is still rare in the UK. The treatment you give your dog for fleas generally works for ticks, but you should discuss the best product to use with your vet.

(see page 163)

Below:
If you have a cat, your dog has a greater chance of picking up fleas.

How to remove a tick

If you spot a tick on your dog, do not try to pluck it off as you risk leaving the hard mouth-parts embedded in his skin. The best way to remove a tick is to use a fine pair of tweezers or you can buy a tick remover. Grasp the tick head firmly and then pull the tick straight out from the skin. If you are using a tick remover, check the instructions, as some recommend a circular twist when pulling. When you have removed the tick, clean the area with mild soap and water.

Ear mites

These parasites live in the outer ear canal. The signs of infestation are a brown, waxy discharge, and your dog will continually shake his head and scratch his ear. If you suspect your Bulldog has ear mites, a visit to the vet will be needed so that medicated ear drops can be prescribed.

Fur mites

These small, white parasites are visible to the naked eye and are often referred to as 'walking dandruff'. They cause a scurfy coat and mild itchiness. However, they are zoonetic – transferable to humans – so prompt treatment with an insecticide prescribed by your vet is essential.

Harvest mites

These are picked up from the undergrowth, and can be seen as a bright orange patch on the webbing between the toes, although this can be found elsewhere on the body, such as on the ear flaps. Treatment is effective with the appropriate insecticide.

Skin mites

There are two types of parasite that burrow into a dog's skin. Demodex canis is transferred from a mother to her pups while they are feeding. Treatment is with a topical preparation, and sometimes antibiotics are needed.

The other skin mite is Sarcoptes scabiei, which causes intense itching and hair loss. It is highly contagious, so all dogs in a household will need to be treated, which involves repeated bathing with a medicated shampoo.

Common ailments

As with all living animals, dogs can be affected by a variety of ailments. Most can be treated effectively after consulting with your vet, who will prescribe appropriate medication and will advise you on how to care for your dog's needs.

Here are some of the more common problems that could affect your Bullldog with advice on how to deal with them.

Anal glands

These are two small sacs on either side of the anus, which produce a dark-brown secretion which dogs use when they mark their territory. The anal glands should empty every time a dog defecates but if they become blocked or impacted, a dog will experience increasing discomfort. He may nibble at his rear end,

or 'scoot' his bottom along the ground to relieve the irritation.

Treatment involves a trip to the vet who will empty the glands manually. It is important to do this without delay or infection may occur.

Dental problems

Good dental hygiene will do much to minimize gum infection and tooth decay. If tartar accumulates to the extent that you cannot remove it by brushing, the vet will need to intervene. In a situation such as this, an anaesthetic will need to be administered so the tartar can be removed manually.

Diarrhoea

There are many reasons why a dog has diarrhoea, but most commonly it is the result of scavenging, a sudden change of diet, or an adverse reaction to a particular type of food. If your dog is suffering from diarrhoea, the first step is to withdraw food for a day.

It is important that he does not dehydrate, so make sure that fresh drinking water is available. However, drinking too much can increase the diarrhoea, which may be accompanied with vomiting, so limit how much he drinks at any one time.

After allowing the stomach to rest, feed a bland diet, such as white fish or chicken with boiled rice for a few days. In most cases, your dog's motions will return to normal and you can resume usual feeding, although this should be done gradually.

However, if this fails to work and the diarrhoea persists for more than a few days, you should consult you vet. Your dog may have an infection which needs to be treated with antibiotics, or the diarrhoea may indicate some other problem which needs expert diagnosis.

Ear infections

The Bulldog has small, rose-shaped ears which fold back. They allow the air to circulate, unlike the ears of drop-eared breeds such as Spaniels, so infection is low-risk. However, they still need to be checked on a regular basis.

A healthy ear is clean with no sign of redness or inflammation, and no evidence of a waxy brown discharge or a foul odour. If you see your dog scratching his ear, shaking his head, or holding one ear at an odd angle, you will need to consult your vet.

The most likely causes are ear mites, an infection, or there may a foreign body, such as a grass seed, trapped in the ear.

Depending on the cause, treatment is with medicated ear drops, possibly containing antibiotics. If a foreign body is suspected, the vet will need to carry out further investigations.

Eye problems

The Bulldog has round eyes which should not be too sunken nor too prominent, which minimises the risk of injury. However, you need to keep a close check and if your Bulldog's eyes look red and sore, he may be suffering from conjunctivitis. This may, or may not be accompanied with a watery or a crusty discharge. Conjunctivitis can be caused by a bacterial or viral

infection, it could be the result of an injury, an adverse reaction to pollen, or a congenital defect.

You will need to consult your vet for a correct diagnosis, but in the case of an infection, treatment with medicated eye drops is effective. For information on breed-related eye problems, see page 185.

Foreign bodies

In the home, puppies – and some older dogs – cannot resist chewing anything that looks interesting. This is can apply to the Bulldog who may have a destructive urge, and with his powerful teeth and jaws, he can shred the unshredable! It is therefore essential that the toys you choose for your dog should be suitably robust to withstand damage.

But bear in mind that children's toys may prove irresistible, and some dogs will chew – and swallow – anything from socks, tights, and any other items from the laundry basket to golf balls and stones from the garden.

Obviously, these items are indigestible and could cause an obstruction in your dog's intestine, which is potentially lethal.

The signs to look for are vomiting, and a tucked up posture. The dog will often be restless and will look as though he is in pain.

In this situation, you must get your dog to the vet without delay, as surgery will be needed to remove the obstruction.

Heatstroke

The Bulldog's head structure, with the short muzzle and flat nose, means that he has a tendency to suffer from respiratory problems. This means that he has a low tolerance to heat and can overheat quickly, resulting in excessive panting and some degree of stress.

If the weather is warm make sure he has access to shady areas, and wait for a cooler part of the day before going for a walk. Be extra careful if you leave your dog in the car, as the temperature can rise dramatically – even on a cloudy day. Heatstroke can happen very rapidly, and unless you are able lower your dog's temperature, it can be fatal.

If your Bulldog appears to be suffering from heatstroke, lie him flat and work at lowering his temperature by spraying him with cool water and covering him with wet towels. As soon as he has made some recovery, take him to the vet where cold intravenous fluids can be administered. For information on breed-related respiratory problems, see page 184.

Lameness / limping

There are a wide variety of reasons why a dog can go lame, from a simple muscle strain, to a fracture, ligament damage, or more complex problems with the joints. If you are concerned about your dog, do not delay in seeking help.

As your Bulldog becomes more elderly, he may suffer from arthritis, which you will see as general stiffness, particularly when he gets up after resting. It will help if you ensure his bed is in a warm draught-free location, and if he gets wet after exercise, you must dry him thoroughly.

If you Bulldog seems to be in pain, consult your vet who will be able to help with pain relief medication.

Skin problems

If your dog is scratching or nibbling at his skin, first check he is free from fleas (see page 168). There are other external parasites which cause itching and hair loss, but you will need a vet to help you find the culprit.

In the summer months when heat and insects are in abundance, your Bulldog might be afflicted by wet eczema, either through a bite or sting, or simply by developing a 'hot spot' and scratching it.

What appears as a small, circular abrasion can, within hours, develop into a red, weeping sore patch the size of a dinner plate if not dealt with immediately. Unfortunately, these 'hot spots' always seem to appear in easily accessible locations: under the collar or around the head and ears – all places which your dog can readily scratch.

Make sure you keep a bottle of liquid antiseptic in the medicine cabinet and liberally douse the affected area with a dilution of this if you notice the smallest sign. Your vet will probably prescribe antibiotics and a cream, but if you are able to contain it at the outset, you may avoid an ugly bare patch which takes a considerable time to disappear.

An allergic reaction can also cause major skin problems, but it can be quite an undertaking to find the cause of the allergy.

You will need to follow your vet's advice, which often requires eliminating specific ingredients from the diet, as well as looking at environmental factors.

Breed-specific disorders

Like all pedigree dogs, the Bulldog has breed-related disorders, which are mostly related to his particular conformation. If diagnosed with any of the diseases listed below, it is important to remember that they can affect offspring, so breeding from affected dogs should be discouraged.

There are now recognised screening tests to enable breeders to check for affected individuals and hence reduce the prevalence of these diseases within the breed.

DNA testing is also becoming more widely available, and as research into the different genetic diseases progresses, more DNA tests are being developed.

Brachycephalic airway obstruction

This affects the Bulldog and other brachycephalic breeds because of the way they are constructed. The foreshortened muzzle and flattened nose, combined with an overlong soft palate, can cause difficulty in breathing. Signs range from snuffling and snorting, a reduced ability to exercises and, in severe cases, collapse.

This is most evident in hot and humid weather so great care should be taken to ensure the Bulldog does not over-exert himself in these conditions.

Congenital deafness

This appears to be linked to the piebald gene, with deafness resulting from degeneration of the blood supply to the cochlea – a spiral shaped cavity in the inner ear – during the first few weeks of life. There are tests available which can be used to assess hearing when a puppy has reached five weeks of age.

Cryptorchidism

This is a condition in male dogs where one or both testicles fail to descend into the scrotum. The testicle or testicles remain within the inguinal canal or within the abdomen, which can cause complications. Surgery is therefore the best option for affected dogs.

Eye disorders

Entropion

Entropion is a condition in which the eyelid turns
inwards, thus scratching the cornea or conjunctiva.

If unattended, this can cause permanent damage
and blindness. It is extremely painful and is easily
detected as the dog will suffer from excessive
blinking and an abundantly watering eye.

Surgery is reasonably straightforward and effective.
Affected dogs should not be used in breeding
programmes.

Keratoconjunctivitis sicca

This condition, also known as 'dry eye' occurs when
there is inadequate tear production.

The eye becomes dry and itchy; the cornea may
become ulcerated and scarred resulting in loss of
vision.

Treatment is geared to stimulating the tear glands
and administering artificial 'tears' for the duration of
the dog's life.

Joint disorders

Congenital luxation

The elbow joint is affected, and the first signs of
lameness are seen in the front limbs when a Bulldog
is around four to five months of age. Surgery is
effective.

Elbow dysplasia

This is caused by a malformation of the elbow
joint and is the most common cause of forelimb
lameness. The condition is diagnosed through X-ray.

Hip dysplasia

This is a degenerative disease that leads to
instability in the hip joint. The bones are often not
held together properly and move apart. This results
in the joint capsule and ligament stretching, adding
further instability in the joint. The signs are pain,
lameness and reduced tolerance to exercise in the
younger dog; older dogs may well be affected by
arthritis in the joint. All potential breeding stock
should be X-rayed and hip-scored.

Patellarluxation

The kneecap (patellar) slips out of place causing the
knee (stifle) to lock so that it is unable to bend. The

characteristic sign is when a Bulldog hops for a few paces and then resumes his normal gait when the patellar goes back to the right position. Surgery may be needed in severe cases but, generally, a Bulldog will live with this condition and be largely unaffected, although arthritis may occur in the stifle in later life.

Mitral valve dysplasia

This is a congenital heart defect; a puppy is born with a malformed heart valve between the two chambers of the left side of the heart which affects its pumping ability. This can vary from being very slight to causing heart failure; a detailed ultrasound examination is needed to assess the extent of the problem.

Summing up

It may give the pet owner cause for concern to find about health problems that may affect their dog. But it is important to bear in mind that acquiring some basic knowledge is an asset, as it will allow you to spot signs of trouble at an early stage. Early diagnosis is very often the means to the most effective treatment. Fortunately, the Bulldog is generally a healthy and disease-free dog with his only visits to the vet being annual check-ups. In most cases, owners can look forward to enjoying many happy years with this outstanding companion.

Useful addresses

Breed & Kennel Clubs
Please contact your Kennel Club to obtain contact information about breed clubs in your area.

UK
The Kennel Club (UK)
1 Clarges Street London, W1J 8AB
Telephone: 0870 606 6750
Fax: 0207 518 1058
Web: www.thekennelclub.org.uk

USA
American Kennel Club (AKC)
5580 Centerview Drive, Raleigh, NC 27606.
Telephone: 919 233 9767
Fax: 919 233 3627
Email: info@akc.org
Web: www.akc.org

United Kennel Club (UKC)
100 E Kilgore Rd, Kalamazoo,
MI 49002-5584, USA.
Tel: 269 343 9020
Fax: 269 343 7037
Web: www.ukcdogs.com

Australia
Australian National Kennel Council (ANKC)
The Australian National Kennel Council is the administrative body for pure breed canine affairs in Australia. It does not, however, deal directly with dog exhibitors, breeders or judges. For information pertaining to breeders, clubs or shows, please contact the relevant State or Territory Body.

International
Fédération Cynologique Internationalé (FCI)
Place Albert 1er, 13, B-6530 Thuin, Belgium.
Tel: +32 71 59.12.38
Fax: +32 71 59.22.29
Web: www.fci.be

Training and behavior
UK
Association of Pet Dog Trainers
Telephone: 01285 810811
Web: www.apdt.co.uk

Canine Behaviour
Association of Pet Behaviour Counsellors
Telephone: 01386 751151
Web: www.apbc.org.uk

USA
Association of Pet Dog Trainers
Tel: 1 800 738 3647
Web: www.apdt.com

American College of Veterinary Behaviorists
Web: dacvb.org

American Veterinary Society of Animal Behavior
Web: www.avsabonline.org

Australia
APDT Australia Inc
Web: www.apdt.com.au

For details of regional behaviorists, contact the relevant State or Territory Controlling Body.

Activities
UK
Agility Club
www.agilityclub.co.uk

British Flyball Association
Telephone: 01628 829623
Web: www.flyball.org.uk

USA
North American Dog Agility Council
Web: www.nadac.com

North American Flyball Association, Inc.
Tel/Fax: 800 318 6312
Web: www.flyball.org

Australia
Agility Dog Association of Australia
Tel: 0423 138 914
Web: www.adaa.com.au

NADAC Australia
Web: www.nadacaustralia.com

Australian Flyball Association
Tel: 0407 337 939
Web: www.flyball.org.au

International
World Canine Freestyle Organisation
Tel: (718) 332-8336
Web: www.worldcaninefreestyle.org

Health
UK
British Small Animal Veterinary Association
Tel: 01452 726700
Web: www.bsava.com

Royal College of Veterinary Surgeons
Tel: 0207 222 2001
Web: www.rcvs.org.uk

www.dogbooksonline.co.uk/healthcare

Alternative Veterinary Medicine Centre
Tel: 01367 710324
Web: www.alternativevet.org

USA
American Veterinary Medical Association
Tel: 800 248 2862
Web: www.avma.org

American College of Veterinary Surgeons
Tel: 301 916 0200
Toll Free: 877 217 2287
Web: www.acvs.org

Canine Eye Registration Foundation
The Veterinary Medical DataBases
1717 Philo Rd, PO Box 3007,
Urbana, IL 61803-3007
Tel: 217-693-4800
Fax: 217-693-4801
Web: www.vmdb.org/cerf.html

Orthopaedic Foundation of Animals
2300 E Nifong Boulevard
Columbia, Missouri, 65201-3806
Tel: 573 442-0418
Fax: 573 875-5073
Web: www.offa.org

American Holistic Veterinary Medical
Association
Tel: 410 569 0795
Web: www.ahvma.org

Australia
Australian Small Animal Veterinary
Association
Tel: 02 9431 5090
Web: www.asava.com.au

Australian Veterinary Association
Tel: 02 9431 5000
Web: www.ava.com.au

Australian College Veterinary Scientists
Tel: 07 3423 2016
Web: acvsc.org.au

Australian Holistic Vets
Web: www.ahv.com.au